GREEN:HOUSE
GREEN:ENGINEERING

Environmental Design at Gardens by the Bay

Patrick Bellew and Meredith Davey of Atelier Ten

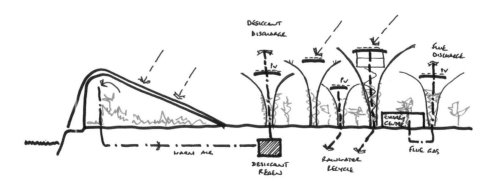

ORO
EDITIONS

Published by
ORO editions
Publishers of Architecture, Art, and Design
Gordon Goff: Publisher
www.oroeditions.com
info@oroeditions.com

Copyright © 2012 by ORO editions
ISBN: 978-1-935935-56-8
10 09 08 07 06 5 4 3 2 1 First edition

With the exception of the list below, all photographs, sections and sketches within the book
are courtesy of Atelier Ten, Grant Associates, Wilkinson Eyre or Atelier One.

Craig Sheppard is credited with the following photographs: front cover, page 10, page 20, page
24, page 28, page 30, page 41, page 58, page 62, page 63, page 65, page 67, page 68, page 69,
page 73, page 80, page 81, page 86, page 89, page 90, page 93, page 96, page100, page103,
page 108

Graphic Design: Davina Tjandra & Pablo Mandel
Edited by: Atelier Ten and ORO editions
Color Separations and Printing: ORO Group Ltd.
Printed in China.

This book was printed and bound using a variety of sustainable manufacturing processes and materials
including soy-based inks, acqueous-based varnish, VOC- and formaldehyde-free glues, and phthalate-free
laminations. The text is printed using offset sheetfed lithographic printing process in 4 color on 157gsm
premium matt art paper with an off-line gloss acqueous spot varnish applied to all photographs.

ORO editions makes a continuous effort to minimize the overall carbon footprint of its publications. As
part of this goal, ORO editions, in association with Global ReLeaf, arranges to plant trees to replace those
used in the manufacturing of the paper produced for its books. Global ReLeaf is an international campaign
run by American Forests, one of the world's oldest nonprofit conservation organizations. Global ReLeaf
is American Forests' education and action program that helps individuals, organizations, agencies, and
corporations improve the local and global environment by planting and caring for trees.

Library of Congress data: pending

For information on our distribution, please visit our website
www.oroeditions

CONTENTS

FOREWORD

Dr. Kiat W. Tan
Advisor to NParks & Chief Executive Officer (Gardens by the Bay)

The Gardens by the Bay project was conceived as a vision anchored on the bedrock of pragmatism. The opportunity to communicate to the community of Singapore the urgency and importance of environment sustainability with its linked message of the value of biodiversity conservation arose from the need to expand the footprint of the business and financial hub of the City. On this prime piece of ocean-front real estate, minted some forty years earlier through land-fill, a new garden to complement the venerable Singapore Botanic Gardens was planned as the green lung to serve the business and residential development that would enclose the open space like a pocket-sized Central Park, indeed a park one-fifth the size of the New York original.

The task to translate the brief to an implementable Masterplan for the Bay South component of the Gardens by the Bay was entrusted to the winner of a highly competitive international competition, Andrew Grant Associates. The brief was ambitious but finely focused. The outcome would embellish Singapore's hard-won reputation as a tropical garden nation and responsible global citizen. More importantly, it would attract a hitherto non-garden frequenting core of citizens who would be drawn by the iconic architecture and arresting infrastructure to enter the domain. Thereafter, the key educational content can be imparted through the unfolding storyline as the gardens are traversed, and by the interpretation of the heritage gardens and the secret world of plants.

The success of this grand enterprise rests on the total understanding of the intent of the project, the creativity and professional talent and skill brought to bear in achieving the technical and aesthetic aspirations, and the passion-driven effort in translating dream into reality. The men and women involved in this implausible journey have risen to the challenge. This unique team comprising individuals representing client, consultant and contractor interests has achieved something wonderful: The Gardens by the Bay.

PREFACE

Patrick Bellew RDI
Principal Atelier Ten

This book tells the story of the evolution and development of the technical systems that make the two conservatories suitable for displaying one of the greatest collections of plants on earth.

Our incredible journey started in November 2005 when Atelier Ten were asked by Andrew Grant to join a team for an invited competition to design a new garden for the city state of Singapore. The proposed team included Wilkinson Eyre Architects for building design and our sister company Atelier One for structural engineering design. The brief, which included two enormous cooled glasshouses at the heart of the scheme, set some very challenging environmental ambitions and it was perhaps the most exciting and ambitious project we had ever encountered. We accepted the invitation without a second thought.

We have worked with Andrew and his team on several projects including the Earth Centre in Doncaster (UK) where their designs proved to be an education in how sustainability and landscaping could come together. We have also worked with architects Wilkinson Eyre on many projects prior to this one, perhaps the most relevant being at the Royal Botanic Gardens, Kew (UK) where we collaborated on the Jodrell Laboratory building and the Alpine House. The latter, although tiny in scale compared to the proposed glasshouses in Singapore, gave us a particular insight into the complex world of providing the optimal "weather" inside a building for plants as opposed to providing environments for people. This insight proved to be vital in the early decision-making stages for Gardens by the Bay.

As the competition design proposal emerged, so our understanding of the scale and complexity of the proposition in front of us grew. Inevitably, the glasshouses are compared to those at the Eden Project in Cornwall (UK), which at the time represented the global benchmark for an environmentally responsible habitat for tropical and other plants within extremely large enclosures. But Singapore offered considerable additional challenges to those experienced in the Eden Project, not least of which was the particularly hot and humid climate of the region and the low-carbon aspirations of the client. We also looked to the Buckminster Fuller inspired "Climatron" in the botanical Gardens of St Louis, Missouri (US) by architects Murphy and Mackey which opened in 1960 and claims to be the first air-conditioned glasshouse in the world.

The design for the Gardens and the structures that evolved through the competition process bears a striking resemblance to the completed project, and many of the environmental concepts that are described in the following pages were developed during the process of the competition design. This arguably serves to demonstrate the often stated view that the most important decisions about the design of buildings are made in the first phase of its evolution. With the exception of the external shading systems and the biofuel powered energy centre, most of the components of the finished project were in place by the time the competition was delivered in mid-2006. The animated video, made by Squint Opera for the competition submission, has proved to be an enduring classic.

A few weeks after the competition judging, we were summoned by Dr Tan's team to a meeting in a London hotel to be told that we had won the competition and that they wanted to be on site within 18-24 months. This started an extraordinary period of intensive research and design work where we collaborated with the client and the design team to evolve the proposals to a point where the buildings could be detailed for tender and construction.

The project represents an amazing fusion of landscape, architecture, structure and environmental design. The leaders of the teams in these respective disciplines were Andrew Grant, Paul Baker, Neil Thomas and myself. In 2008, we realised that in the space of a few months we would all reach the significant milestone of our 50th birthdays and the "200 Club" was formed to celebrate this happy coincidence. While this may seem frivolous, it is symptomatic of the intensity of the collaboration that we were engaged in. The authors are grateful to Andrew, Paul and Neil for their contribution to this publication, for their insights and above all for their continual friendship.

opposite The Alpine House at Kew Gardens, a collaboration between Wilkinson Eyre and Atelier Ten

below Early imaging renderings of the interior of the Flower Dome

opposite Early visual for the Cloud Forest

Many people at Atelier Ten contributed to the detailed analysis of the buildings and to the design of the environmental systems but I have to single out Meredith Davey as being instrumental in the success of our part of the project. He led the competition team and worked tirelessly with National Parks Board of Singapore and the wider team to develop and deliver the analysis and assessments that were the key to the engineering design. I am enormously grateful to him for his contribution. Also huge thanks to Piers Watts-Jones who led the coordination and integration of the extremely complex central energy systems and became so deeply involved in the thermodynamics of the processes that we sometimes wondered whether he ever slept. He also spent a great deal of time in Singapore during the construction ensuring that our partner engineers at CPG and the contractors fully understood the nuances of the systems.

CPG also had a significant role to play in delivering the final working drawings for the buildings and the systems and for the infrastructure in the Gardens. They also managed the engineering installation work during the construction phase and their contribution to the delivery of the project is gratefully acknowledged.

Thousands of construction workers, engineers and landscapers toiled in the heat and humidity of Singapore to build and assemble what we had conceived and drawn; our efforts pale into insignificance compared to theirs in getting these extraordinary gardens and buildings constructed in such a relatively short time.

Sincere thanks to my co-author Meredith Davey for his significant contribution to the writing in this book, and to Nick Schofield, Seohaa Lucas-Choi and Leanne Renn of Atelier Ten for their support and assistance in pulling this project together and again to Seohaa for her wonderful graphics that grace these pages. It would not have happened without their persistence and organisation. This was truly a team effort. Inspiration comes from many places, particularly from collaborators and colleagues. This book is dedicated to my wife Lois and my children Zoë, Ruaraidh and Freya - the greatest inspirations in my life.

A UNIQUE CHALLENGE

A UNIQUE CHALLENGE

The Gardens by the Bay is part of a major citywide initiative by the National Parks Board of Singapore (NParks) in their plan to move from being a Garden City to a City in a Garden. The total project is made up of three significant new urban gardens around the Marina Bay area, the first of which, Marina Bay South, is the largest. Bay South comprises a landscaped garden and water system covering an area of 54 hectares (134 acres) built on partially reclaimed ground in the estuary mouth of the Singapore River on a site that includes two significant rainwater run-off channels that link the land to the south with the Bay.

The project was the subject of an invited international design competition organised by NParks in 2006. Their aim was to find an innovative and implementable masterplan design for the Gardens. The Bay South competition was won by a team led by Andrew Grant of Grant Associates, involving Wilkinson Eyre Architects and Atelier One, with Atelier Ten as environmental designers and building services engineers.

The design was commissioned in 2006 and the Flower Dome and a portion of the gardens opened as a preview to the public in November 2011. The Gardens opened formally to the public in June 2012. The project includes two large cooled conservatories or 'biomes' with a footprint of 20,000m² at the north-eastern end of the gardens and eighteen large 'Supertree' structures, ranging from 25m to 50m in height, arranged in three clusters around the conservatory complex. The two conservatories were known throughout the design stage as the Cool Dry Biome and the Cool Moist Biome. They were renamed the Flower Dome and the Cloud Forest as the project moved towards opening day.

The Flower Dome re-creates the conditions in Mediterranean spring time with mild, dry days and cool nights. It is 170m long, 86m wide and 38m high, contained within a clear spanning double glazed gridshell structure.

The Cloud Forest Dome emulates the conditions of mountainous tropical regions: areas where the air temperature is relatively mild during the day and slightly cooler at night but with humidity levels that are approaching saturation throughout both the day and night. The Cloud Forest Dome is 118m long, 77m wide and 58m high and has a large mountain in the centre with aerial walkways to take visitors through

The masterplan for the 54Ha
Marina Bay South Gardens by Grant
Associates showing all elements of
Phases 1 and 2 ©Grant Associates

The Marina Bay Sands complex
is on the west side, the Barrage
is at the Eastern End. The
Conservatories are on the North
bank, facing Marina Bay

The environmental diagram showing sustainability cycles that was developed for the competition submission by Grant Associates. It incorporates the energy, water and materials cycles and illustrates the role of the supertrees in the environmental system

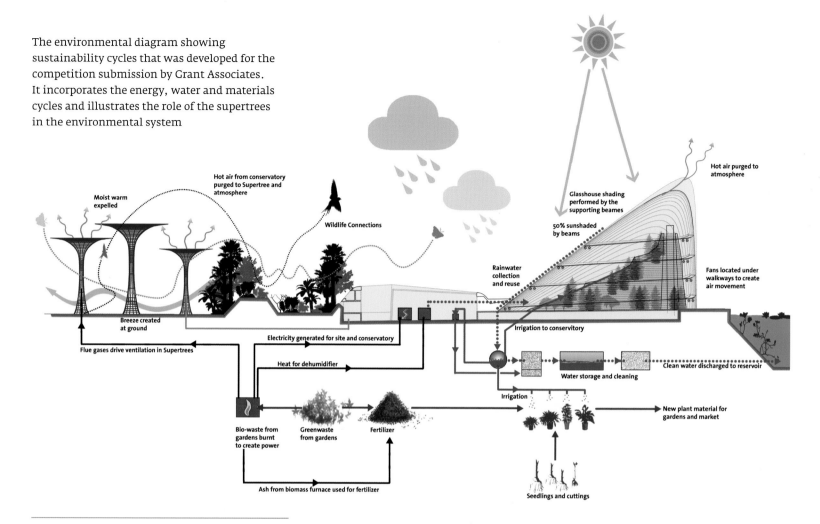

The project illustrates how design optimisation and cross-discipline integration can result in high-performance, responsive buildings even in very demanding climatic conditions and, with a highly technical and challenging environmental design brief.

the tree-tops. The Supertrees support many of the environmental systems associated with energy production and ventilation of the glasshouses as well as supporting vertical gardens, providing a focal point to the gardens and shade for visitors.

Each biome has a number of unconventional design requirements in order to create artificial environments and allow plants from Mediterranean and Tropical Montane regions to flourish in the tropical climate of Singapore. The project illustrates how design optimisation and cross-discipline integration can result in high-performance, responsive buildings even in very demanding climatic conditions and with a highly technical and challenging environmental design brief.

The project is concerned with recreating nature; the elements for the development have been interleaved to create an enhanced ecosystem for the site, with the conservatories and the gardens being designed to be symbiotic through the interaction of energy, water, nutrient and water cycles and processes.

above The Eden Project in Cornwall, England

The Eden Project, Cornwall, UK

The Eden Project complex in Cornwall, UK which opened in March 2001 is dominated by two large enclosures consisting of adjoining domes that house thousands of plant species, and each enclosure emulates a natural biome. The first dome emulates a tropical environment and the second a Mediterranean environment. The structures are of a similar size to the cooled conservatories at Gardens by the Bay and serve similar functions.

The structure is completely self-supporting, with no internal supports, and takes the form of a geodesic structure: each dome consists of hundreds of hexagonal and pentagonal, inflated plastic cells supported by steel frames. The external cladding panels are made from the thermoplastic ETFE. Each panel is made from several layers of thin UV-transparent ETFE film sealed around their perimeter and inflated to create a large cushion. The resulting cushion acts as a thermal blanket to the structure.

This was an appropriate solution for a temperate climate but the ETFE material is not well suited to the tropical and equatorial conditions at Gardens by the Bay. The main lessons learned from Eden related to the daylighting levels for the plants. This is described in detail later.

MASTERPLAN
SITE WIDE STRATEGIES

The Andrew Grant Masterplan structures the design of the public garden on the organisation and physiology of the Orchid, the national flower of Singapore. Andrew describes in the following section how this garden structure evolved and developed from an early concept to finished garden of extraordinary scale and complexity.

An early decision that was key to the evolution of the plan related to the placement of the conservatory buildings within the gardens. A future extension is planned to the Singapore financial centre on the sites around the gardens. This development will involve several tall buildings which could potentially cast shadows over the southern and eastern borders of the garden site. The recently completed Marina Bay Sands Hotel, with its iconic rooftop pool and garden complex, already casts a significant shadow across the centre of the site in the afternoon. The conservatories require as much light as possible and their location was carefully selected in the area of the site adjacent to the Bay to guarantee that it receives the highest solar exposure and daylight even once these surrounding buildings are developed.

right View of the Gardens from the north-east with the glasshouses in the foreground. The Masterplan located the glasshouses on the edge of the bay to reduce shading impacts from the Marina Bay Sands Hotel

As the design evolved, the main plant and equipment to service the buildings was located in an energy centre to the south of the conservatory cluster, in a zone of the gardens that also houses a number of support buildings and an additional support glasshouse.

A key ambition was to make the servicing of the conservatories as invisible as possible and in particular to avoid surrounding them with air intakes, louvres, chillers or visible air handling plant. As the design evolved, the main plant and equipment to service the buildings was located in an energy centre to the south of the conservatory cluster, in a zone of the gardens that also houses a number of support buildings and an additional support glasshouse. Hot and 'dirty' air discharge and renewable energy provisions are dealt with via the Supertrees and the various components are interconnected by service tunnels, which also serve as interconnections for back-of-house activities.

The Masterplan paid considerable attention to creating sustainable water cycles. The site sits on the edge of Marina Bay which was until recently a tidal estuary but has been turned into a fresh water marina and reserve by the construction of a new barrage to the east of the site. In developing the Masterplan, key concepts of water retention, conservation and purification were incorporated into the design. Direct rainfall from within the site catchment is filtered and cleansed of nitrogen, phosphorus and suspended solids arising from the gardens operation, prior to discharge into the Marina Reservoir.

right Looking north from the Dragonfly bridge. The boardwalk and planting beyond are a part of the water cleansing system

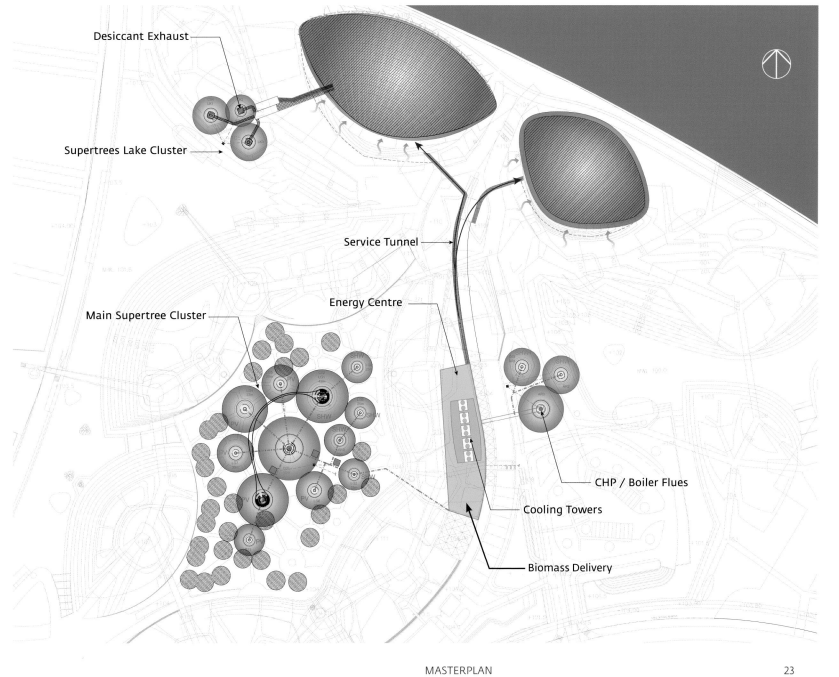

Desiccant Exhaust

Supertrees Lake Cluster

Service Tunnel

Main Supertree Cluster

Energy Centre

CHP / Boiler Flues

Cooling Towers

Biomass Delivery

The intermittent and 'peaky' nature of tropical storms makes this a complex task of retention and release, and the solution uses aquatic landscapes to remediate the received water through a series of inter-connected lakes and filter ponds and planting troughs. The filter ponds leading into the lake are formed from a number of different layers of permeable substrate to allow the incoming water to be naturally filtered, without the need for mechanical filtration equipment. Further treatment is undertaken in a sustainable manner through the use of aquatic plants within the water bodies.

To support the planting on the site and within the conservatories, a comprehensive irrigation system has been installed. This ensures the plants can be watered when there is either insufficient rainfall or the plants are located in areas that do not receive direct rain fall. The purified water within the Dragonfly Lake, running along the north-west boundary of the site, is used as a naturally replenished water source. A large submersed tunnel leads from the deepest point of the lake into an open well formed in the plant room at the rear of the Flower Dome conservatory. Water from this well is distributed by a network of pipes to the planting on the site by an intelligent automated irrigation system which responds to climatic conditions.

Water sensitive urban design strategies were further developed and detailed with water quality models, for incorporation into the gardens' design. Much of this was undertaken by Grant Associates and NParks, together with CPG Consultants and Cardno.

above The energy centre sits between the entrance Plaza and the Lion Grove food court. The circular elements on top of the energy centre are the cooling tower exhausts. In the foreground the solar panels on top of the Supertrees can be seen

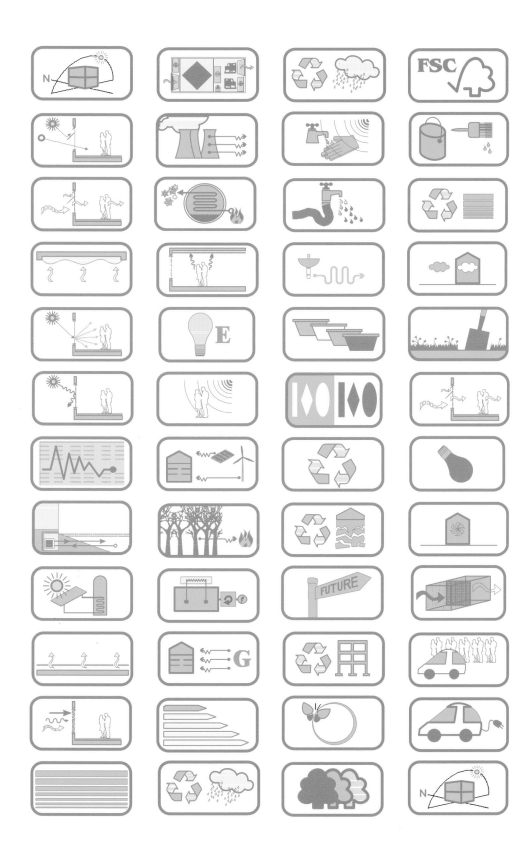

Sustainability & Benchmarking Implementation Plan

As part of the Masterplan development and implementation process, Atelier Ten developed and utilised a range of sustainability implementation plans (SIP's) for the development tailored to the different teams delivering the various parts of the project. These covered all areas of environmental sustainability potentially affected by the development, and aimed to weave holistic ideas of sustainability into the project. Benchmarking of the sustainability initiatives on the project is through the Singapore's Building & Construction Authority (BCA) Green Mark scheme. The BCA Green Mark scheme is a Singaporean equivalent of LEED™ in the US or BREEAM in the UK and is a comprehensive gauge of a developments sustainability measures. The conservatories have received a Platinum rating and the Marina South development as a whole is on track for Platinum certification.

MASTERPLAN AND GARDEN STRATEGY

Andrew Grant of Grant Associates

This project is about the plants. Specifically, to allow the full appreciation of their forms, colours, textures, functions and ultimately, their importance to us as humans in the 21st century. NParks have sourced plants from across the planet to create a unique botanical reservoir and a visual and sensory spectacle. At this moment this incredible collection of botanical diversity is just taking root and hinting at the magnificence to come over the next 100 years and more.

In addition to permanent planting displays and collections of rare species, the gardens feature temporary displays. Maintenance is an essential part of the garden story and is implicit in the clients' desire to explore new boundaries in horticulture. Nevertheless, the whole aspect of environmental sustainability has been a central theme of the design evolution including going to considerable lengths to ensure an efficient energy strategy for the cooled conservatories and the creation of a unique reservoir of South East Asian Rainforest species.

This competition winning idea structures the design of the 54 hectare public garden on the organisation and physiology of the orchid. The orchid is the National flower of Singapore and is the most cosmopolitan species of flowering plant in the world. At the same time it is typically epiphytic or transient in its colonisation of habitats. It seemed to us entirely appropriate to capture the essential qualities and characteristics of orchids in the layout and underlying philosophy for these new gardens.

The sketches show a progression of the idea. First the garden takes root on a piece of new garden infrastructure and grows out from the waterfront towards the city. Leaves (earthworks) and roots (water, energy, communication systems) and shoots (paths, roads and links) create an integrated network across the space and beautiful flowers (feature/theme gardens) occur at key intersections or nodes.

The Masterplan has evolved from these simple ideas into a highly sophisticated and integrated 3D network of horticulture, art, engineering and architecture. It is chasing the idea of creating a highly distinctive and decorative garden landscape underpinned by serious engineering of environmental infrastructure and world-class garden architecture. This holistic vision is captured in the concept diagram of the garden ecosystem.

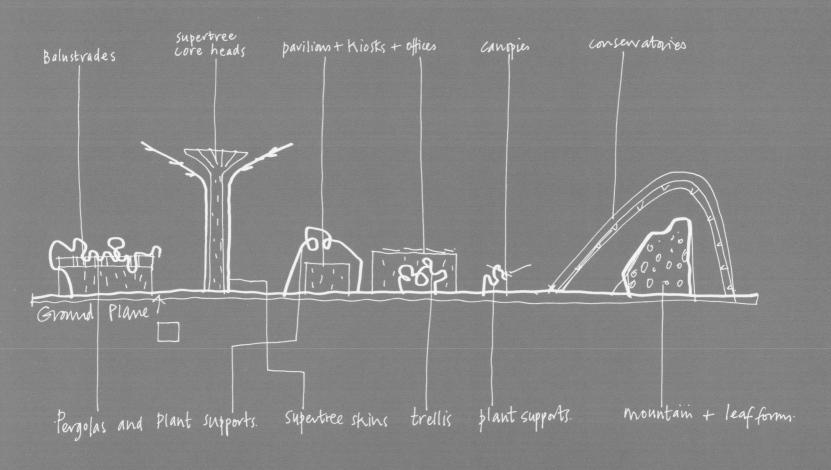

Balustrades

supertree
core heads

pavilions + Kiosks + offices

canopies

conservatories

Ground Plane

Pergolas and Plant supports.

Supertree skins

trellis

plant supports.

mountain + leaf form.

Singapore
Architecture + Garden Structures.
9/7/08

The Supertrees

At the heart of the gardens are the 'Supertrees'. They are a rare fusion of design, nature and technology. They evoke science fiction and yet are tangible and real, enormous and expressive in scale form and colour. We always saw the Supertrees as a distinctly landscape counterpoint to the massive conservatories. Without the Supertrees the gardens would just be about the conservatories with a series of gardens and planting attached. The Supertrees change the centre of gravity of Bay South and announce the true heart of the gardens.

The idea and feel for the Supertrees was in part inspired by the 'Valley of the Giants' in SW Australia. I visited these amazing trees when I went to see my brother who lives near Perth. The striking experience of changing from the normal eucalyptus forest into the super tall worlds of the Karri trees along with the experience of the elevated walkway was very inspiring. We merged this physical reference with the magical experience of the forest seen in the Studio Ghibli film Princess Mononoke to create the character and scale of the Supertree Grove.

above The main Supertree cluster at the heart of the site. The 50m Supertree in the centre houses a two-storey bar and access to the aerial walkway

GREEN:HOUSE GREEN:ENGINEERING

The Biomes

The conservatory landscape strategy was to create two contrasting experiences and internal environments. The Flower Dome was to be the 'Theatre of Plants' with the emphasis on the colours, scents and flowers of the Mediterranean world, while the Cloud Forest Dome was to be an immersive vertical journey through a biodiverse, lush and exotic cloud forest.

Apart from scale and spectacle of the spaces, the designs have tried hard to make sure these conservatories are not just about botanical collections of plants but are enriched with other functions and experiences. The Flower Dome houses a number of function spaces and restaurants which take advantage of the amazing botanical setting. The Cloud Forest Dome integrates leading edge multi-media interpretation to reinforce the educational background to the project.

The Gardens

The Gardens are designed to offer a wide range of outdoor leisure opportunities but an underlying thematic concept holds the designs together and provides a framework for a significant educational experience. The gardens are divided into three principal zones; Heritage Gardens which is concerned with the plant associations of the four man cultural groups of Singapore, Indian, Chinese, Malay and Western. World of Plants which is concerned with the biodiversity and beauty of a S.E. Asian Rainforest. And Natures Balance which explores the integration of art, science and nature. A number of specific themed gardens illustrate these principles through planting displays and interpretation.

In addition, the wider landscapes include shaded walks through recreated Rainforest or alongside the Dragon Fly Lake. The main Events Lawn offers a space for large outdoor concerts and community events while the Supertree Grove at the heart of the Gardens is a unique tropical garden enclave during the day and a spectacular and magical night garden destination.

Planting

The client, NParks, is a leading authority on tropical horticulture and a key objective of the project from the outset has been to explore the potential for new and different types of planting design through this project. NParks has scoured the world to find new and interesting plant species that have never been planted in Singapore before. The collections of Baobabs, bromeliads and aquatic planting displays will be of particular interest. A design challenge has been to find ways of introducing extensive colour using flowers and coloured foliage. In addition there is a great emphasis on biodiversity and the recreation of S.E.Asian habitats. An extensive plant nursery has been established by NParks where large trees have been salvaged from development sites and prepared for the gardens.

Green Walls and Vertical Planting

The project includes extensive use of green walls both internally and externally. They are of three main types. Geotextile Reinforced Earth Walls help to define spaces and offer a way of softening steep slopes that might otherwise be developed as concrete walls. Vertical planting panels offer a more refined framework for planting on vertical surfaces including the Supertrees and selected walls. 'Living Render' provides a porous and roughly textured concrete surface that incorporates a proportion of organic material in the concrete mix to create moisture retention and rooting zones for epiphytes. The Mountain in the Cloud Forest Dome will be a major display of this Living Render technique.

Stones and Rocks

A feature of the landscape is the use of distinctive stones as focal points and highlights within the planting. These have been sourced from around the region with the most spectacular coming from China.

Mangosteen Colour Palette

Grant Associates and Thomas Mathews graphic designers developed a site wide colour, signage and wayfinding strategy. This uses the colours of the Mangosteen fruit as the basis for the palette including a dark purple as the principal unifying colour highlighted by the contrasting greens, oranges and whites. In addition, the themed gardens are defined by colours associated with the cultures of Singapore and the colours of the rainforest. The rich claret of the Supertrees and the bright red of the dragonfly bridge add to this overall colour composition. In addition to the colour palette, a branding pattern has been developed inspired by the flora and fauna of Singapore.

opposite left The structural fins of the Flower Dome as seen from the bay edge

opposite right Both Biomes with the shading deployed to protect from the strong afternoon sun

THE ENVIRONMENTAL BRIEF

THE ENVIRONMENTAL BRIEF

In the competition brief NParks provided high-level but somewhat limited briefing information to the bidding teams about the two environments that were to be provided within the conservatories. To generate the competition submission the team drew on their experiences of designing other glasshouses and systems for hot humid climates to develop an appropriate, logical and efficient environmental response. These included the use of high-performance double glazing on the façades, solar powered desiccant air drying, variable shading to the façades and the first evolution of the virtuous cycle diagram.

NParks were aware from their monitoring of a relatively small cool moist glasshouse in the existing Botanical Gardens that to provide the desired temperature ranges using conventional dehumidification and cooling strategies would be very energy intensive and prohibitively expensive to run. In preparation for the Bay South project, they ran a research project for several years with the German climate engineers, Transsolar (Stuttgart) and CPG Consultants (Singapore) to assess the required growing conditions for the target species for the biomes developing a detailed final briefing document that was provided to the competition winning

The weather in Singapore

Singapore (latitude of 1.37ºN) exhibits a conventional equatorial tropical climate being hot and humid throughout the year with relatively small seasonal and diurnal temperature variations. Approximately 95% of hours are between 24°C and 32°C with moisture content between 17-21 g/kg.

Being close to the equator, direct solar radiation is very intense in clear sky conditions with peak vertical irradiance intensities in excess of 1050 W/m² and with high levels of diffuse sky radiation. There is however a tendency for heavy cloud cover with overcast skies for long periods, and the sky luminance levels in these conditions can be low for longer periods than might be experienced in a typical Mediterranean summer, an important consideration when developing the daylighting strategy for the buildings.

Psychrometric Chart
showing climatic classifications and Singapore weather data

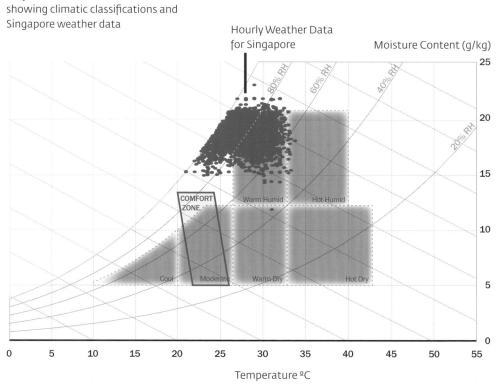

right View across the flower dome to the baobab trees. The target daylight level within the glasshouses is 45,000 lux

team. At the time of the competition they had designed and were constructing six prototype glasshouses on the edge of the city to allow detailed study of the behaviour of plants under glass. The outcomes of their research and early experiments were used to inform and shape the environmental design brief for the conservatories, and resulted in further refinement and optimisation of the competition proposals to meet this challenging brief document.

The prototype glasshouses were constructed while the design stage for Gardens by the Bay was in process. They tested different glass specifications, shading and equipment specifications and investigated the resulting effect on plant growth.

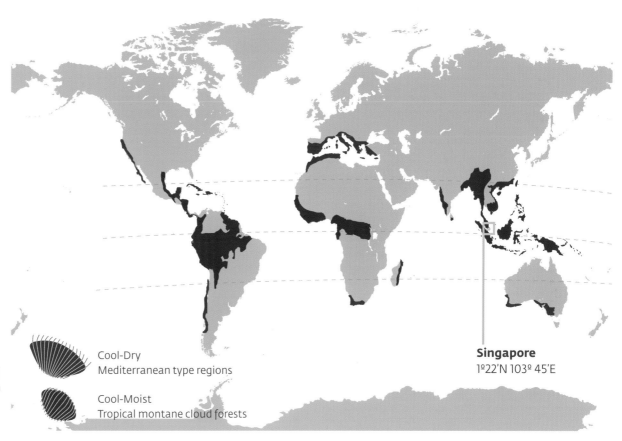

right Geographic locations of species to be contained within the two Biomes

Cool-Dry
Mediterranean type regions

Cool-Moist
Tropical montane cloud forests

Singapore
1º22'N 103º 45'E

Light levels

Identifying annual and peak light levels to support plant growth was a key requirement. Research indicated that a peak illuminance level of 45,000 lux was important for plant growth of key groups of flora that would form a part of the display within the buildings. This target figure was benchmarked to the Eden Project in Cornwall where similar flora has flourished. NParks research determined that levels greater than 45,000 lux do not benefit growth, longevity or the quality of the plants. Light levels and solar heat gains are inevitably connected via the properties of the glass façade and any excess light would lead to an unnecessary increase to the cooling load in the biome, which was already going to be challenging. (45,000 lux is some 100 times brighter than would normally be provided in an office environment.)

Frequency spectrum

NParks research demonstrated that plant growth of different species is highly dependent on light levels in the visible spectrum but less dependent on levels at the IR and UV wavelengths. Plants requiring supplementary UV radiation could, if necessary, be 'dosed' with occasional UV from horticultural lamps but such dosing would not be essential to their growth. Cladding material selection could therefore prioritise visible light (390 - 750µm) over other frequencies.

Lux Level
Comparing spaces

Internal Illuminance Level (Lux)

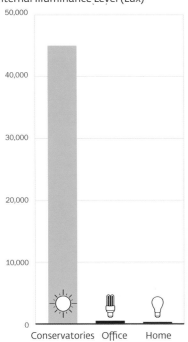

Solar Spectrum

Spectral Irradiance (W/m²/nm)

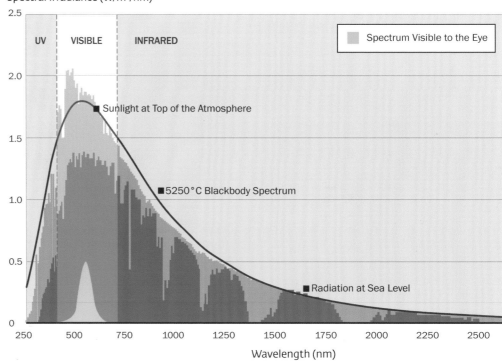

As part of the technical brief developed by NParks there were specific temperature and humidity conditions to be achieved inside each of the conservatories, in addition to light requirements. Rather than having static conditions, the brief called for the temperatures and humidity to vary throughout the day, and over months as well, to simulate the plant's experience within the natural habitats that they originate from. These design conditions are superimposed on the psychrometric chart below. This chart also shows annual external design conditions superimposed as dots representing hourly measurements. From this chart, it can be seen there is no single hour of the year, day or night, when natural ventilation or the introduction of untreated air would be an option for the conditioning strategy. Some conditioning of the outdoor air would always be needed (the points on the chart where the external air is cooler than the "Cloud Forest – Day Condition" occur at night when the design point is lower). The chart also illustrates the principal challenge which was to achieve cooling and dehumidification in an energy efficient way.

Psychrometric Chart
Location: Singapore IWEC

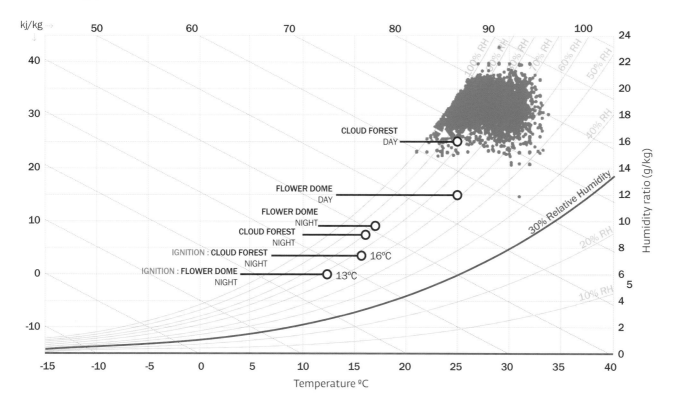

GREEN:HOUSE GREEN:ENGINEERING

Thermal conditions

The target design condition for the air inside the Flower Dome during the day is 25°C, at a relative humidity (RH) of 60%. During the night this is reduced to 17°C with 80% RH. Every third month, for every night in the month, the night time temperature is lowered to 13°C, to signal to the plants that the winter has passed and that they should spread their flowers for spring. This process is known as "Ignition" and 13°C is known as the Ignition Temperature. In the Cloud Forest Dome, the temperature regime is broadly similar to the Flower Dome but the moisture content is significantly different. During the daytime the design condition is 25°C at 80% RH or higher. This is approximately 4g/kg more moisture embodied in the air or approximately 10kJ/kg higher enthalpy in the atmosphere compared to the Flower Dome. During the night this is lowered to a temperature of 17°C at 80% RH. Again for nights during one month in every three, the temperature is reduced within this biome to 16°C at 80% RH for Ignition.

Human comfort was also a significant consideration. Comfort responses in the human body are complex and the design solutions were calibrated by reference to 'environmental' or 'operative' temperature requirements that include an assessment of the radiant heat environment as well as the air temperature and relative humidity. While operative temperatures were considered, the final design for air flows and conditioning was based on air temperature. This decision was taken following agreement by NParks to the external shading solution that included individual control and variability to each shade. This dramatically reduced the radiant temperature on sunny days and gave control over the radiant temperature environment.

Through the competition briefing and the subsequent brief development stage, the Client actively encouraged the design team to consider innovative design solutions to minimise energy consumption and carbon emissions. In addition, the environmentally aware Mah Bow Tan, Minister for National Development until May 2011, who was responsible for championing the project through the planning and fundraising process, specifically instructed that the team should endeavour to make the carbon emissions from the systems conditioning the buildings no worse than would be experienced in a modern Singapore office building of the same total floor area. This was a significant challenge, but one that was achieved and exceeded by the final design.

UNDERSTANDING
THE ARCHITECTURAL INTENT

Paul Baker of Wilkinson Eyre Architects

Although Wilkinson Eyre's approach has always promoted the idea of collaboration between technical and artistic disciplines, we had never before worked on a project which demanded from the outset such a thorough integration of skills as that for Gardens by the Bay. In putting together the team, Andrew Grant of Grant Associates had selected practices which not only had experience of working together, but whose design approach combined a commitment to the environment with an instinctive understanding of placemaking.

In 2002, Wilkinson Eyre developed a new Masterplan for the Royal Botanic Gardens Kew in London. This set out a framework for future development across the site, including both public buildings and scientific facilities for the organisation's extensive programme of plant research. We then delivered several of the projects within the Masterplan, including an extension to the Jodrell Laboratory and a new Alpine House. It was these projects that cemented our creative relationship with Atelier Ten.

The Jodrell Laboratory extension was a reasonably straightforward project: a new, timber-clad wing to an existing building with a simple yet effective strategy for passive environmental control developed from first principles. Tucked away from the public face of the gardens it made a quiet and much-needed addition to Kew's research accommodation. The second project, however – the Davies Alpine House – had a higher profile, and a far more complex brief. Alpine plants are exposed to high levels of sunlight at altitude but do not overheat because they are exposed to constant winds. Therefore they require high light levels, cool conditions and continual air movement for successful growth. Atelier Ten's innovative environmental solution, based on principles observed in nature in a termite's nest, closely informed our architecture – which subsequently went on to win a handful of design awards and much media interest. With an elegant twin-arched form, the glasshouse encloses a relatively tall internal space for its footprint, enabling a stack effect to occur which draws cool air from an underground labyrinth. By working together to create a glasshouse which – in contrast to usual examples of its

type - creates a cool growing environment within rather than a warm one, we had pre-empted one of the central challenges of the Singapore brief.

From the earliest competition stages, the team's vision was to create gardens and structures which were mutually supportive, taking a holistic view of the site rather than considering the key buildings simply as objects placed onto the landscape. The cooled conservatories were conceived as an integral part of this wider garden ecosystem. They capture the landscape below them, transforming it to create growing environments dramatically different to Singapore's own humid tropical climate, and simulating nature at work by working in tandem with other structures across the gardens to minimise energy use.

For us, it was Patrick Bellew, Meredith Davey and their team at Atelier Ten who brought unique insight and innovation to this environmental vision. During the course of the project, which over six years involved many extended trips together to Singapore, the time spent in their company was always entertaining and fun – and thought provoking in the way that a simple three-hour design meeting never can be. Being away from the office gave us many informal opportunities to throw ideas around about the design, and the space to really develop and refine them.

Atelier Ten's thinking on the environmental strategy was integral to the development of the design for the conservatories, although their form began at Wilkinson Eyre as a more organic sketch which brought together the climate-controlled biomes required by the brief in a fluid cluster on the prominent waterfront edge of the site. We were very conscious that their presence on Marina Bay would become part of the city's visual identity, the picture postcard view of Singapore, and so envisaged them as organic landforms, adding a new element to the composition of landmarks around the bay, and contrasting sharply with the dense urban development on the northern shore. Their position also anticipates future development around the gardens to avoid

For us Gardens by the Bay represented a unique opportunity: to work with an exceptionally engaged and visionary client to fulfil an incredible brief, and alongside consultants who shared with us a commitment to true collaboration.

potential overshadowing by nearby tall buildings.

Just as at Kew we found that the principal design challenge was the conflicting need to maintain the high light levels required by the plants (in the Flower Dome from Mediterranean climate zones, and in the Cloud Forest biome from cool tropical forests) within while minimising the associated solar heat gain inevitable in Singapore's tropical climate. We therefore took a tiered approach, achieving as much environmental control as possible through passive means before resorting to more energy-hungry active systems.

Firstly, the complementary yet distinct curved forms of the biomes are generated from the geometry of a hyperbolic curve, and so contain a large volume within a relatively small surface area. Not only does this geometry enable the structure to be optimised (allowing a lightweight, column free interior), it also works well environmentally, creating a stack effect with warm air drawn up to stratify according to temperature within the space. The gentle forward tilt of the Flower Dome towards Marina Bay also shades the north façade so it never receives the full glare of the sun.

The envelope is also critical to the success of the system. With the structure designed to be as lightweight as possible to

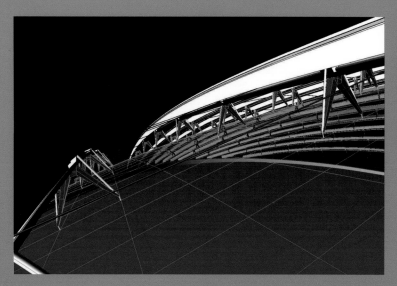
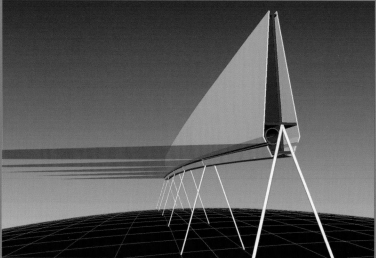

minimise shadows cast onto the planting below, highly selective glass is used to filter out as much heat from the sun as possible. Deployable shades concealed within the structural arches of the building are also used to control the light levels and limit heat gain.

And inside, just as at the Alpine House but on a much grander scale, cool air is delivered into the building at low velocity, trickling into the planted displays and collecting in pockets of the undulating internal landscape to provide the right growing conditions for the plants as well as comfort to visitors. Above the cooled, inhabited levels, the warmer air collects and creative a reservoir at the top of the dome. This hot air is collected from the top of both conservatories and, along with surplus heat from the on-site biomass boiler, is used to regenerate a desiccant by driving off the moisture.

This stepped approach, developed in collaboration with Atelier Ten, represents the kind of sustainable specificity at the heart of this once-in-a-lifetime project. For us, Gardens by the Bay represented a unique opportunity: to work with an exceptionally engaged and visionary client to fulfil an incredible brief, and alongside consultants who shared with us a commitment to true collaboration.

opposite Computer renderings of shading system deployment. Note that the north elevation is largely self-shading by virtue of the angle (Courtesy of Wilkinson Eyre)

top The cleaning crew on the outside of the Flower Dome show the scale of the sail-like external shades

bottom The automatic shades in the flower dome under test before opening

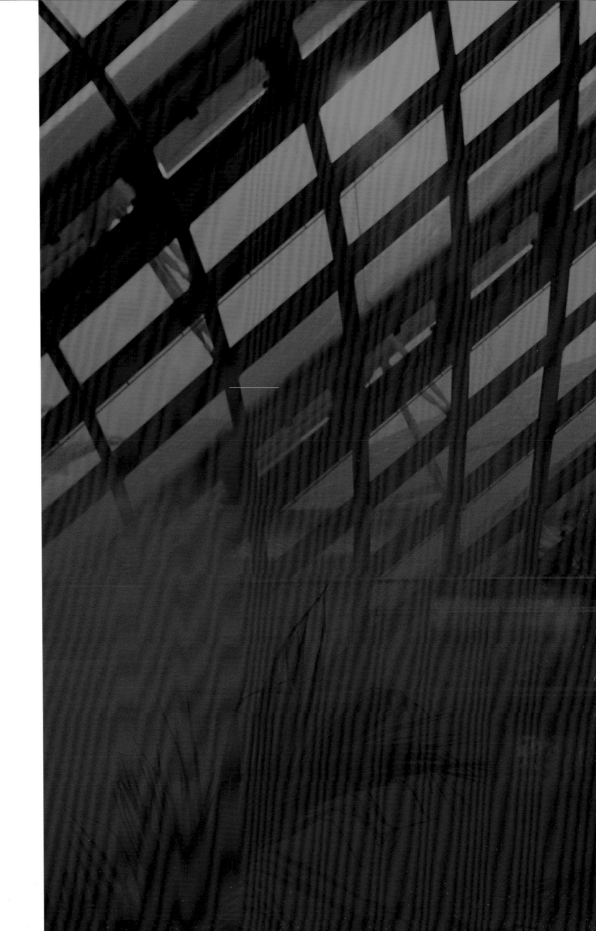

INTEGRATED DESIGN

BIOME STRUCTURE, ENVELOPE
& BUILDING SERVICES

INTEGRATED DESIGN
BIOME STRUCTURE, ENVELOPE & BUILDING SERVICES

The design of the systems for ventilation, cooling and dehumidification did not begin in earnest until the relationship between horticultural lighting requirements, solar gain and cooling load were fully understood and modelled. The brief for the external envelope of the structures was that they should be sufficiently transparent to visible light to achieve the 45,000 lux (described earlier) for at least as many hours in a year as are achieved in the biomes at the Eden Project.

Singapore is a notoriously cloudy place and during the frequent periods with dense cloud cover the light levels can be very subdued; but there are also long periods of intense equatorial sunshine when skies are clear. Balancing daylight levels and frequencies with thermal requirements was one of the major challenges faced by the design team.

Extensive analysis was undertaken on the structure and envelope to optimise it for natural daylight penetration and solar control to ensure that the building delivered sufficient daylight for the range of planting proposed for the biomes. The competition winning scheme had worked on an assumption that some combination of optimised glazing transparency with the primary steel structural beams acting as fixed shading elements would be sufficient to provide daylight control and limit excess solar gains. The structure was originally conceived as solid fins with the glazing suspended beneath in a simple mullion system.

As the analysis work progressed this proved to be too simplistic an assumption. The deep structure obscured too much of the sky vault in cloudy and low-light situations but was also not effective in dealing with high levels of solar heat gain at times when the sunlight is normal to the glazed surface. This would have led to comfort issues for occupants and more cooling load than could reasonably be met by practical and discreet cooling systems. The main structural members were deliberately placed outside the glazing to help with shading, they have a clear span of up to 120m in places and so were of considerable depth.

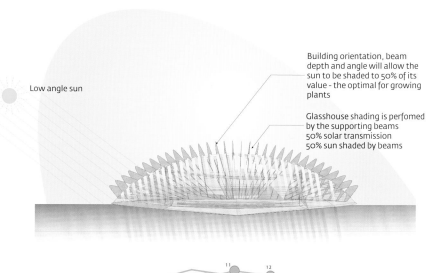

Low angle sun

Building orientation, beam depth and angle will allow the sun to be shaded to 50% of its value - the optimal for growing plants

Glasshouse shading is perfomed by the supporting beams
50% solar transmission
50% sun shaded by beams

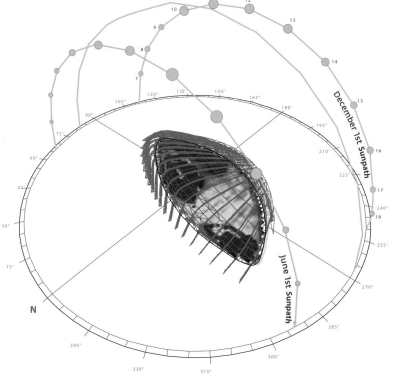

opposite top Competition sketch showing main structure envisaged as primary shade

opposite bottom Singapore sunpath diagram superimposed on annual daylighting study of gridshell structure option

Balancing daylight levels and frequencies with thermal requirements was one of the major challenges faced by the design team.

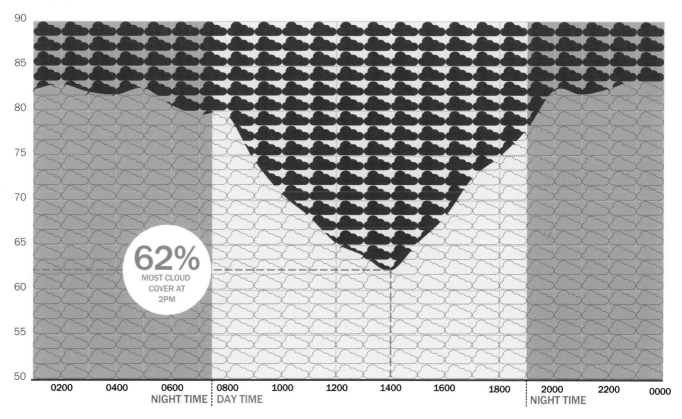

Cloud Cover
Represented as annual percentage of sky vault visible at time

% of sky vault visible

Time of day

Diagram showing the percentage of the sky obscured by clouds during daylight hours. This data was vital to understand the climate that the buildings were going to experience, and in particular the frequency of overcast vs. clear skies in Singapore

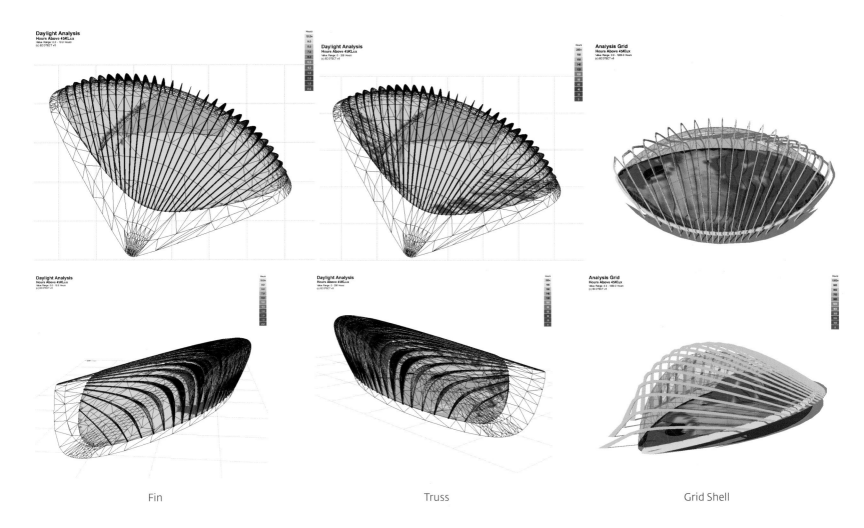

Fin   Truss   Grid Shell

above Output from cladding optimisation studies of the fin structure option (left), the bowstring truss option (centre) and gridshell option with external beams (right) ©Atelier Ten

right Early architects rendering ©Wilkinson Eyre

The question was whether this arrangement would obscure too much of the incident light in the course of a year and, if so, what were the alternative structural arrangements that could improve the performance? Advanced daylight simulation techniques were used to assess the availability and quantity of daylight for the entire inhabited volume for each hour of a typical year for a number of different structural solutions including:

- an optimised solid fin design with non-structural secondary glazing elements (competition scheme)
- an external truss system also with non-structural secondary glazing elements
- a grid shell to hold the glazing tied to more slender primary arches.

The optimisation process included the assessment of both the peak and cumulative annual illuminance levels and the frequency of achieved illuminance levels across the whole floor plate for each of the options. The analysis was performed using a combination of proprietary software (Ecotect and Radiance were the main tools) and bespoke software generated by us for the project, to evaluate and filter the output data from the models and compare it with the Eden Project data.

The analysis showed that the reduction in daylight from the primary and secondary structural elements was significant but that the restrained grid shell option offered the best balance of daylight and solar control. It also turned out to be the most cost and material effective solution to deliver the enclosure.

With the frequency of dense cloud cover in Singapore, the analysis also showed that the glazing selected would need to have a high degree of transparency to daylight to meet the target daylight requirements. As infra-red radiation from the sun carries a lot of heat but was found not to benefit the plants, the glazing did not have to have the same degree of transparency to the infra-red spectrum of solar energy as to visible light. With the need for high daylight transmission, the use of body tinting of the glass was not an option and so selective coatings were investigated as the preferred option.

It was evident from the outset that with the intensity of the tropical sun it would be essential to have class-leading levels of frequency selectivity built into the glass. A review of glazing performance and market availability around the world was carried out to find the best trade-off between light transparency and infra-red (heat) reflection to ensure that the cladding was specified with the best achievable performance.

This is a summary of our analysis of the daylight levels (in lux) for the Flower Dome. It illustrates a prediction (yellow line) of the number of hours that the daylight levels (on the X axis) are exceeded at the internal planting level for the final gridshell structural cladding option. This prediction is compared with the conditions in the Eden Biome to verify performance against the brief

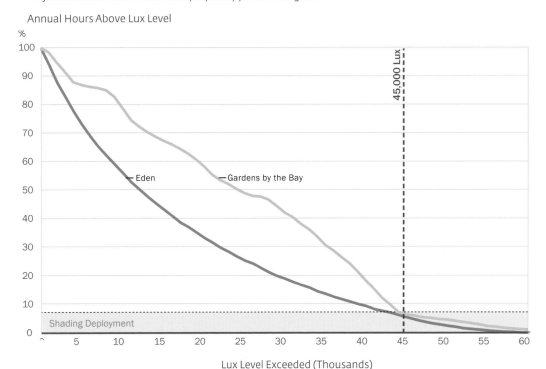

Modelling Shading Impacts
Projected Illumination Levels and frequency for 65% VLT glass

Annual Hours Above Lux Level

A review of glazing performance and market availability around the world was carried out to find the best trade-off between light transparency and infrared (heat) reflection to ensure that the cladding was specified with the best achievable performance.

CONVENTIONAL GLAZING

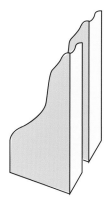

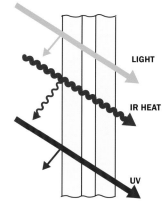

LIGHT

IR HEAT

UV

- Lets as much heat as light through
- Little UV shading

SELECTIVE GLAZING LAMINATE

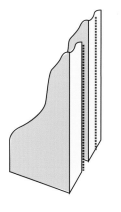

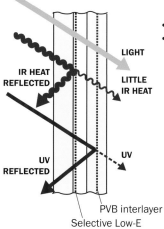

IR HEAT
REFLECTED

LIGHT

LITTLE
IR HEAT

UV
REFLECTED

UV

PVB interlayer
Selective Low-E

- Lets more light through than heat
- Filter UV radiation

Single glazing would have been preferred on the grounds of cost, weight and ease of construction but could not provide the desired selective radiant energy filtration properties with a durable coating solution. There were also significant concerns about the risk of the glasshouses being continually shrouded in a layer of condensation externally if they were clad in single glazing. Single glazing is highly conductive and would have been at a similar temperature on both internal and external surfaces. The temperature of the external glass surface would therefore have been below the 'dew-point' of the external air for the majority of the year, resulting in the formation of condensation. Such condensation would have been particularly evident on cloudy days (the sunshine would evaporate it on sunny days) which would have exacerbated the issue of daylight levels in cloudy conditions; apart from the aesthetic and operational issues of constant condensation.

ETFE, which was used at the Eden Project, was also considered as it offered significant weight benefits. Our analysis demonstrated that although it is a very efficient material in many ways, the coatings were not sufficiently developed to reliably achieve the levels of selective solar energy reflection that high-performance glass could achieve. This would have resulted in a solution with significantly increased cooling loads, air supply requirements and energy consumption.

Double glazing to control radiant transmission and surface temperatures was therefore determined to be a necessity. A specification evolved based on a selective double glazed unit which allows approximately 65% of the incident daylight frequencies to pass through with only 35% of the solar heat transferred, primarily by filtering the infra-red frequencies from passing into the space. This selectivity is achieved by a low-emissivity coating that is applied to the inner face of the double glazed unit's outer sheet of glass. The coating effectively acts as a mirror to the incident infrared light from the sun, reducing unwanted 'heat' from the radiant energy spectrum. Placing this coating on the inside of the outer sheet allows absorbed heat on the coating to be transmitted by convection to the external air rather than to the interior. A number of manufacturers from Europe, North America and Asia were able to meet the specification for this special glass.

Comparing glazing solar heat transmittances and visible light transmittances

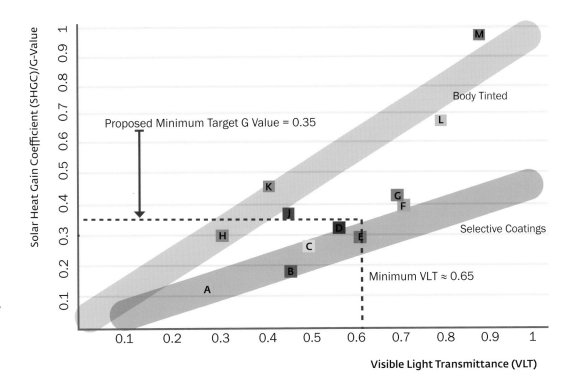

This is a summary of our analysis of daylight levels (in lux) for the Cool Dry Biome. It illustrates a prediction (yellow line) of the number of hours that the daylight levels (on the X axis) are exceeded at the internal planting level for the final gridshell structural cladding option. This prediction is compared with the conditions in the Eden biome to verify performance against the brief

Simulation of Shading Impacts
Frequency of shade deployment

Internal Illuminance Level (Lux)

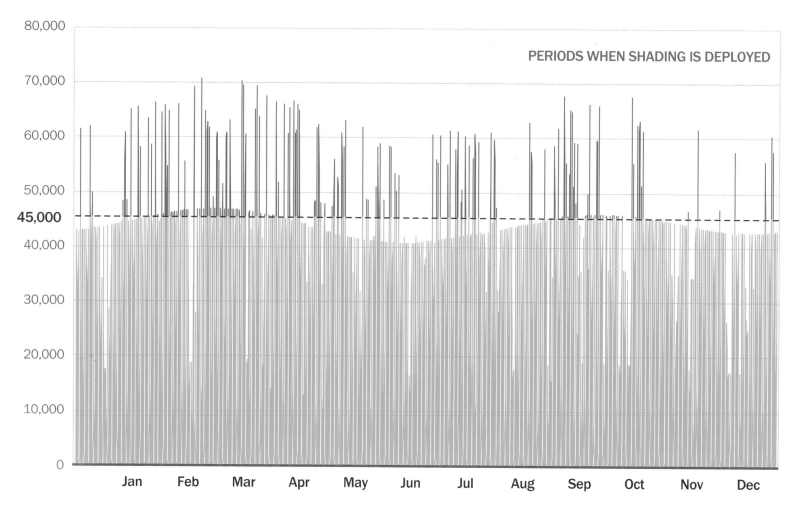

PERIODS WHEN SHADING IS DEPLOYED

GREEN:HOUSE GREEN:ENGINEERING

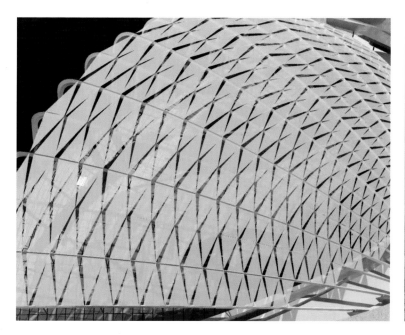

Before this type of selective glass coating was available, designers and architects had to rely on the tinting of glass to control solar heat gain. This effectively reduced the radiant energy transmission across the whole energy spectrum affecting light and heat in more or less equal measure. The availability of selective coatings allows the façade to be visually 'transparent' while being much more opaque to infra-red (heat) radiation.

However, the studies showed that there were many occasions when more light would reach the space than necessary to meet the horticultural requirements. These occasions would generally be coincident with peak solar gains on cloudless days, and can occur at any time of the day. Adjusting the performance of the glass to deal with these peak situations would have resulted in too much loss of light during the frequent periods with lower ambient light conditions to meet the annual average illuminance criteria. There were also concerns that the internal environmental (comfort) temperature would be elevated during periods of high external solar radiation to a point where human comfort would be poor despite the controlled air temperature. This could only realistically be improved by introducing a barrier to sunlight in the form of shading.

Internal shading behind the high-performance glazing units would have trapped heat at high level and while it would have achieved the improvement in comfort and radiation that the design required, it would have required a significantly larger cooling and fresh air system to remove the heat at high level.

Many alternatives for internal and external shading of the glass were considered and sketched. External shading was preferred as it would result in lower overall heat gain, and therefore reduced cooling loads and energy consumption, by keeping the radiant energy outside the building envelope. Internal shading behind the high-performance glazing units would have trapped heat at high level and, while it would have achieved the improvement in comfort and radiation that the design required, it would have required a significantly larger cooling and fresh air system to remove the heat at high level. Maintenance of either external or internal shading would be challenging, access to the external option was deemed less disruptive to plants, visitors and operations and could be achieved from the external building maintenance unit required for cleaning the external façade.

above This is a summary of the expected daylight levels received internally throughout the year, alongside the shading deployment. It illustrates the time (x-axis) against the received lux levels (y-axis) and provides a compressed representation of each hour of the year. When the daylight level is above 45,000lux there is limited horticultural benefit and it is these periods that the shading deploys proportionally to limit the daylight levels inside to 45,000lux. The green lines indicate the periods and intensity of the sun that is shaded in these conditions.

External shading was preferred as it would result in lower overall heat gain, and therefore reduced cooling loads and energy consumption, by keeping the radiant energy outside the building envelope. The shading reduces cooling loss by more than 40% when partially deployed and 70% when fully deployed.

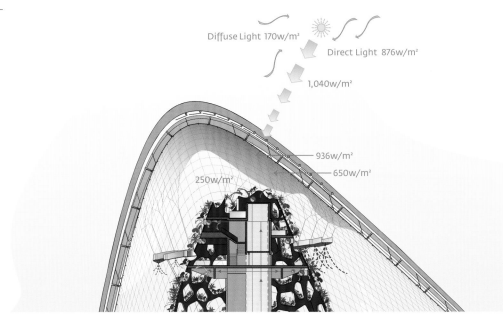

With Shades Deployed

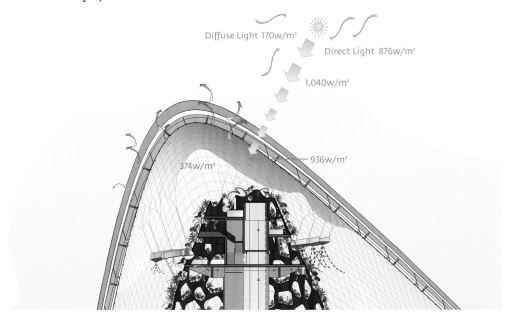

Without Shading

top Quantity of direct and diffuse solar radiation entering conservatory without external solar shading (per m² of glass)

bottom Quantity of direct and diffuse radiation entering conservatory with external shading (per m² of glass)

opposite Walkway within the Cloud Forest

The dynamic nature of the completed building, with the shades opening and closing in response to the changing solar environment is one of the great successes of the completed project.

Wilkinson Eyre Architects came up with a system of retractable external shades that elegantly meet the shading needs. The shades are triangular in form, like sails, and are cable tensioned. They are completely concealed within the lower section of the ribs when not in use and are actively controlled to deploy when required to modulate internal daylight levels to the desired level. As well as improving occupant comfort they reduce the peak cooling demands and save energy by reducing the solar thermal heat transmitted when light levels are satisfied.

The dynamic nature of the completed building, with the shades opening and closing in response to the changing solar environment is one of the great successes of the completed project. A simple and comprehensible message to visitors about the management of energy flows within the building. It is also beautiful in its simplicity.

The internal light levels with and without shades deployed were modelled for a complete reference year to test how frequently the shades would be required.

Each of the 419 external shades are individually variably controllable, with an intelligent self-learning algorithm to adjust the shades to meet the internal daylight levels while responding to the geometry of the internal spaces, the external cladding and the sun-path overhead. The shading system can also be managed to shade walkways inside the building at particular times of day, if this should prove desirable. The shading system also provides additional resilience in case of system failure, as the shades can be deployed in an emergency to reduce solar cooling loads inside the building.

From the earliest competition stages, the biome forms were optimised to allow maximum daylight penetration. The form of the Flower Dome was modified to create an overhang to the north façade, which slopes backwards from a peak. This creates a glass face that is inclined outwards at near the same angle as the peak annual radiation for that orientation at the extreme sun angle and hence is a completely self-shading façade, requiring no external shades.

BUILDING SYSTEMS

AN ENGINEERING RESPONSE

BUILDING SYSTEMS
AN ENGINEERING RESPONSE

Despite the efficiency of the high-performance glass and
the use of external shades during times of high solar gain, there
remained a significant amount of solar and other heat gains into the
biomes that needed to be offset through the introduction of cooling
in various forms. The development of the systems for environmental
control in the buildings began with a number of early conceptual
decisions which were made at the competition stage based on
experience, research and engineering intuition. These drove the
analysis and the design development. These decisions included:

- the use of a displacement air supply system. This involves
  introducing the conditioning air at low level within the
  occupied zone to limit the volume of the building that requires
  conditioning thereby reducing plant capacities and energy use.
  Displacement ventilation also allows for the conditioning supply
  air to be supplied to the space at around 18°C rather than at
  12°C, which would be the norm for a conventional conditioning
  system, and this elevated supply temperature results in
  significant energy savings

- the use of radiant cooling in pathways and pavements within the
  biomes to absorb and remove incident absorbed solar radiation.
  This reduces the amount of heat gain to be dealt with by the air
  systems and reduces mean radiant temperature for occupants,
  improving comfort

- the use of a desiccant dehumidification system to remove
  the need for refrigeration-based dehumidification of air. The
  desiccant regeneration process would allow waste heat to be
  used as a regeneration source

- the use of direct evaporative humidification (misting) within
  the Cloud Forest Dome to provide the very high humidity levels
  required and enhance cooling performance

As a result, the main conditioning method for both biomes is via a displacement ventilation air conditioning. The system uses dehumidified fresh and recirculated air supplied from air handling units located in large plant rooms beneath and to the rear of the biomes. Fresh air is drawn in from outside through air intake louvres and shafts concealed within the embankment planting. Diffusers integrated into the vertical surfaces of the planter beds and displacement diffuser terminals placed in beds throughout each biome deliver air at low velocity into the space at the lowest level.

opposite top Radiant cooling pipework being installed on the upper deck of the flower dome

opposite bottom The main fresh air inlets to the Flower Dome are carefully concealed within the landscape on the perimeter embankment above the air handling plant room. Beneath the louvre is a large sump to catch the frequent heavy rainfall

left Planter beds within the Flower Dome under construction. The vertical elements projecting from the floor are the air supply connections to the displacement terminals. In this area the main air ducts run beneath the planters

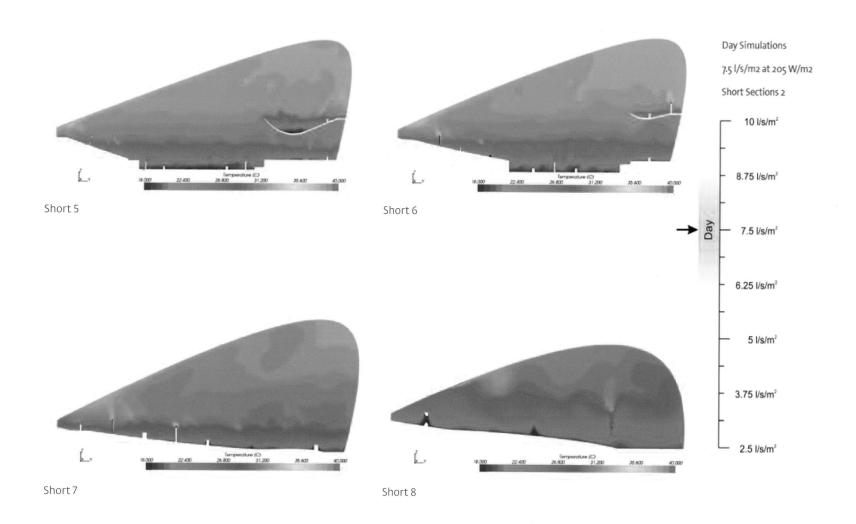

Short 5

Short 6

Day Simulations

7.5 l/s/m2 at 205 W/m2

Short Sections 2

— 10 l/s/m²

— 8.75 l/s/m²

→ Day — 7.5 l/s/m²

— 6.25 l/s/m²

— 5 l/s/m²

— 3.75 l/s/m²

— 2.5 l/s/m²

Short 7

Short 8

Determining the necessary air supply and modelling how it would be distributed through the biomes was a significant challenge. Initial calculations were done using dynamic thermal energy models to predict peak heat gains and mass flow balances to estimate flow rates. Subsequently, computational fluid dynamics (CFD) modelling was used as an iterative design tool to analyse and optimise the air flows into the biomes. The modelling technique used numerous calibrated heat sources to represent re-radiating solar heat gain and internal gains from people. The resultant thermal 'plumes' mimic the absorption and release of radiant heat and can be clearly seen in some of the output sections as detailed above.

opposite Output sections from CFD modeling

bottom Model for displacement ventilation

bottom right Interior shot of Cloud Forest and the mountain top

Multiple studies of different air supply rates were used to determine the optimal ventilation rate based upon the predicted internal stratification of temperature within each building. Ventilation rates, and the consequent thermal stratification, were determined as appropriate for both human comfort and the specific horticultural requirements of both biomes, with an iterative process of review between the designers and the horticulturalists to ensure that the conditions predicted were acceptable. Tests were also carried out with and without external standing devices to prove the necessity under peak load.

The early CFD studies identified that the air surrounding the mountain within the Cloud Forest Dome (which contains a number of open levels inside the mountain) would become hotter than acceptable at high level if it was conditioned by a pure displacement system. As a result, a hybrid ventilation system was developed; this supplies air through displacement terminals at the bottom of the building and at the top of the mountain but at intermediate levels within the mountain, jet diffusers are used to drive local mixing thus limiting the localised stratification. Above the mountain, the air is allowed to stratify, as in a displacement system, before being extracted and re-circulated back to the basement plant. Sealed "black box" rooms inside the mountain use conventional overhead conditioning as these spaces do not connect to the main volume.

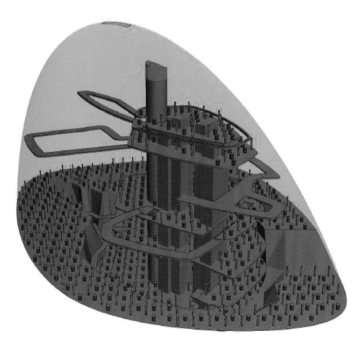

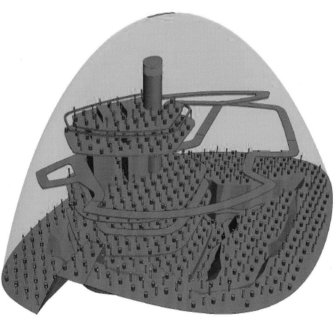

1 Diffuser behind architectural finish
2 Supply air duct from plant rooms
3 Service runs combined into structure
4 Chilled floor to absorb some solar gain
5 Displacement air supply via vertical surface

One of the most complex tasks in the engineering of the domes was the integration and distribution of the air diffusers into the planter beds. The amount of air delivered is very significant, and the ducts were large and needed to be concealed within the soil depth without compromising the depth of soil for the planting above them. Extensive works were undertaken to integrate these air supplies into the buildings in such a way as to be discrete and to ensure that the planting would thrive. In order to achieve the air distribution a number of voids and tunnels were formed beneath the planter beds and the buildings themselves, to allow for a network of ducts to be installed, connecting the air supplies from the plant rooms at the rear of the building to the planter beds.

Floating Walkways
• Supply air distributed via walkways
• Distribution above floor structure
• Adaptation to gradients
• Continuous or individual vents

below left Under construction - this view of the Flower Dome shows the 'barcode' planter walls with their air inlets and the displacement drums within the planters

below right Typical planter bed showing the drum type air displacement diffusers within the planting

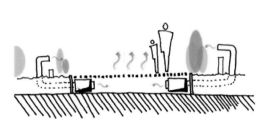

Umbilical Walkways

- Supply air distributed via walkways
- Distribution above floor structure
- Plug-in distribution for localised control or buffeting
- Adaptation to gradients
- Continuous or individual vents

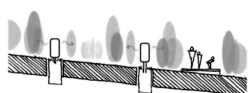

Floating Walkways

- Supply air distributed via walkways
- Distribution above floor structure
- Plug-in distribution for localised control or buffeting
- Adaptation to gradients
- Continuous low-profile vents
- Fixed walkways adaptable to surrounding changes

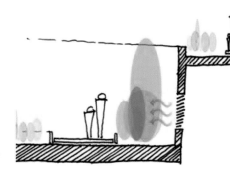

Terraces

- Discreet outlets in terraces and side walls
- Distribution above floor structure
- Fixed or track type arrangement
- Fixed or flexible locations

The biomes are positively pressurised to approximately 10% overpressure through the introduction of fresh air mixed in with the air supply at low level. Excess air is discharged to the atmosphere via operable glazing panels at the top of the structure while the warm air, from close to the top of the biomes, is returned to the basement plant room. Air at the top of the biomes will normally have a higher enthalpy than the ambient external condition because of the height of the buildings and the amount of stratification. Heat recovery would not therefore have been beneficial in the exhaust air stream.

above Windows at the top of the building double as pressure relief vents for the overpressure that is designed into the air supply system to regulate moist air infiltration. The external shades run above the vents and retract into the slots in the bottom of the primary structural beams

left On the upper level of the Boabab Leaf in the Flower Dome, the air supply diffusers are at low-level. The large concrete tube in the background is the main return air duct

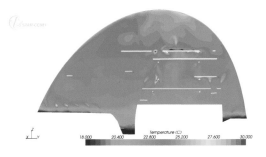

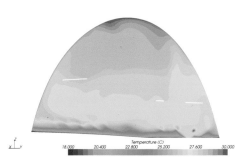

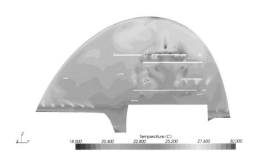

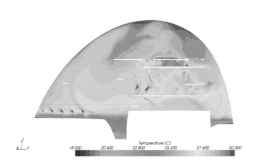

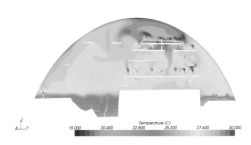

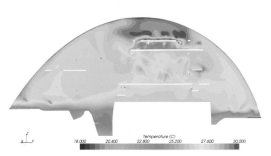

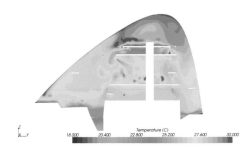

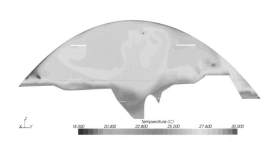

left Early design studies of potential air introduction methods. The final design incorporated variations on these options. These 3D computational fluid dynamic studies of the Flower Dome were used to verify stratification effects at different air supply rates during periods of high solar gain. They demonstrate how the air within the Flower Dome is allowed to vary in temperature vertically to reduce overall cooling levels. The images represent vertical slices through the building at different points.

The next set of studies of the evolved design showed that inducing air from jet nozzle diffusers at intermediate levels within the mountain structure would supress thermal stratification and improve conditions for plants and human comfort.

Cloud Forest Dome displacement ventilation CFD study. This demonstrates that the stratification over the height is unacceptable for the horticultural requirements of the space. These CFD studies of four sections through the Cloud Forest demonstrated that the stratification in the building would lead to unacceptable temperatures in the upper level of the 'mountain' and for the planting surrounding the mountain. An alternative 'hybrid' mode of operation was developed in response. ©Atelier Ten.

opposite Waterfall Cloud Forest

The Cloud Forest Dome requires extremely high levels of moisture to replicate the cool humidity of a high-altitude cloud forest. This could not be achieved through the supply air arrangement described above as it would have required the air to be supplied at more than 100% relative humidity. This is not technically possible. As such, direct evaporative misters were installed within the space to provide additional moisture to the atmosphere. These also provide an evaporative cooling effect. These systems are largely installed within the planting and on the aerial walkways that extend from the mountain. The misters allow moisture to be directly injected into the space to keep humidity levels exceptionally high, but also to form part of the visitor show by creating a visible fog bank inside the building. It was important that the air around the mountain was not too fast moving, with the exception of a few key localised areas to add some of the experience of climbing a real mountain, in order to ensure that the proposed fog would not disperse too quickly.

The horticultural brief required the temperatures within the biomes to be changeable at different times of day and at different times of year to replicate conditions in the wild. In particular these variations activate the reproduction cycles of the plants through a process of 'ignition' at the lower temperatures as described previously. This change in temperature is achieved by varying the chilled water supply temperatures to the biomes at night to allow the air temperature to be modulated to low levels. Varying the temperature in this way results in energy savings through being able to run the chillers at higher evaporating temperatures during daytime operation when the largest cooling loads are experienced

The systems had to be versatile and responsive to meet the large range of internal space conditions under the variable external conditions. Additional CFD modelling was undertaken by the engineering contractor to independently verify that the final arrangement and disposition of air terminals within the glasshouses had been designed appropriately.

left In the Ravine of the Cloud Forest dome looking up at the vertiginous aerial walkways. The walkways incorporate misting nozzles to generate a haze and increase humidity at regular intervals

right top At low-level in the Cloud Forest, the misters hard at work

right bottom In the Cloud Forest Ravine with the Mountain shrouded in mist

FRESH AIR CONDITIONING

USING DESICCANTS

FRESH AIR CONDITIONING
USING DESICCANTS

Drying air in the tropics for delivery to buildings using conventional refrigeration techniques is a very energy intensive activity and a key priority was finding a means of removing moisture that could use solar energy or waste heat processes.

Drying air in the tropics for delivery to buildings using conventional refrigeration techniques is a very energy intensive activity and a key priority was finding a means of removing moisture that could use solar energy or a waste heat processes.

The fresh air supplied to the biomes needs to be at a lower moisture content than the external air of Singapore to achieve the desired internal moisture content. At the competition stage, it was proposed that desiccant technology might offer a way of reducing the carbon impact of the dehumidification process. This proposal was borne out by the work already undertaken by NParks on their prototype conservatories with Transsolar and CPG Consultants.

Desiccant conditioning systems work by directly removing moisture from air streams through a chemical process, usually by using the water absorbent qualities of materials that are composed of salts. These materials can also be liquids: in effect very strong solutions of salty water which are so salty they absorb water from air that passes through a spray of these solutions. As part of a desiccant process, removing water from air results in air heating up (it's the reverse of evaporative cooling), but by coupling the salt solution to free cooling from a cooling tower, the vast majority of this heat can be absorbed without additional energy expenditure. This results in a liquid that absorbs water vapour and increases in volume, leaving the air at a similar temperature but drier.

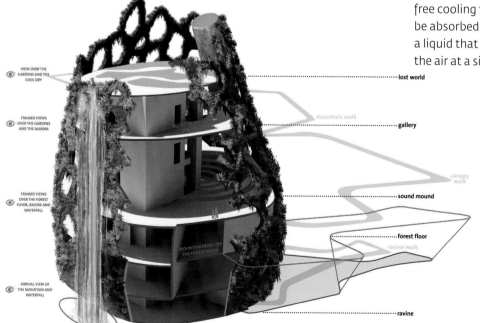

left Section through Cloud Forest Dome

opposite Graphic highlighting desiccant cycle

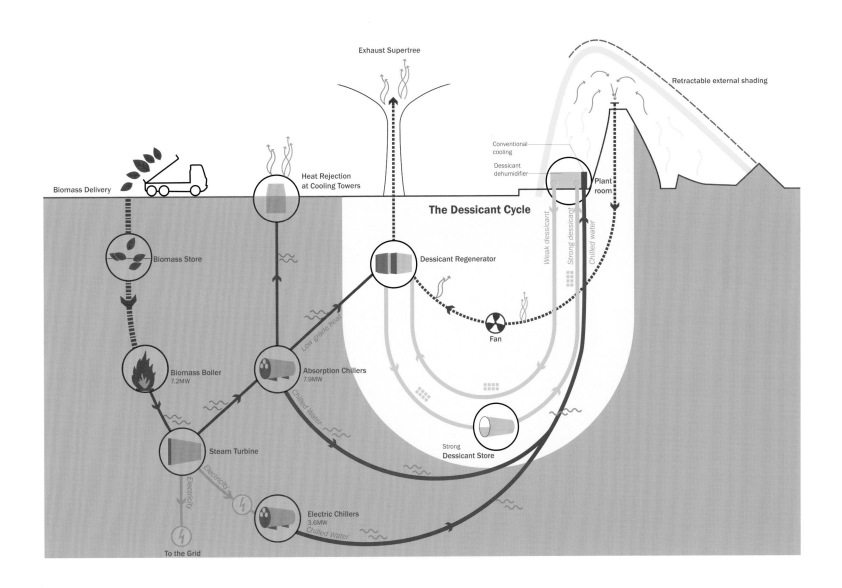

Exhaust Supertree

Retractable external shading

Biomass Delivery

Heat Rejection
at Cooling Towers

Conventional
cooling

Dessicant
dehumidifier

Plant
room

Biomass Store

The Dessicant Cycle

Weak dessicant

Strong dessicant

Chilled water

Dessicant Regenerator

Biomass Boiler
7.2MW

Absorption Chillers
7.9MW

Low grade heat

Fan

Chilled Water

Steam Turbine

Strong
Dessicant Store

Electricity

Electricity

Electric Chillers
3.6MW
Chilled Water

To the Grid

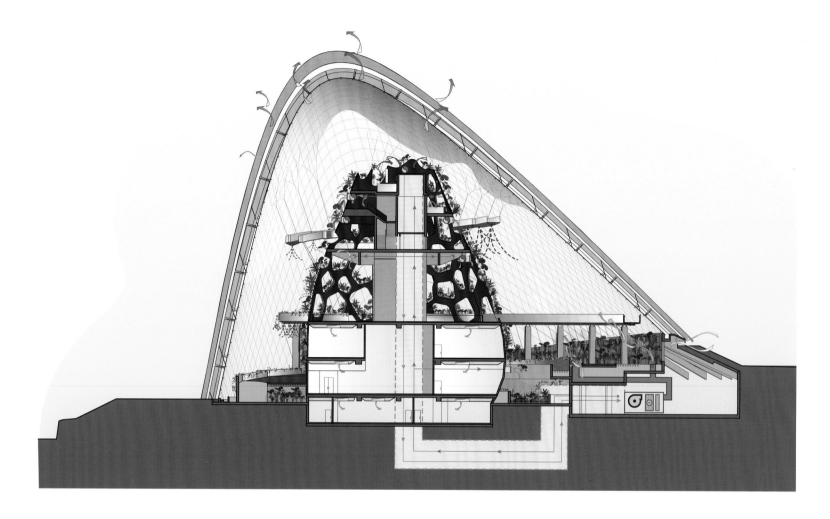

When combined with conventional cooling, liquid desiccant technology allows air to be supplied to a controlled psychometric point (i.e. cooled and dehumidified) with less energy consumption than a conventional approach. A conventional system would over-cool the air supply using chilled water to remove the water vapour by condensation, followed by reheating the air to achieve the required psychometric state.

Desiccant dehumidification processes remove moisture from the fresh air stream while maintaining constant enthalpy (heat). This process increases the temperature of the air stream initially but the resulting drier airstream is easier to cool using a 'sensible' cooling process to reach the desired design condition without the overcooling

and reheating. Liquid desiccants were preferred over the more familiar solid type because of the size of the installation and due to the complexity involved in juxtaposing supply and extract airstreams which is necessary when using solid desiccants.

Lithium Chloride was selected as the preferred desiccant for the project. A highly concentrated 'strong' solution of Lithium Chloride dissolved in water extracts moisture from an air stream when the two are brought into contact either over a surface doused with the solution or through a curtain of solution sprayed into the air stream. The moisture removed from the humid air increases the volume of the desiccant solution as it is absorbed: it also removes the majority of microbiological contamination in the treated air stream.

right An early diagram used in the exploration and explanation of the liquid desiccant cycle and its relationship to the central energy plant. At this stage we were researching a fuel cell as the primary energy source for the site. This was subsequently modified to the biomass CHP system described in the following pages

opposite Environmental section of Cloud Forest Dome showing ventilation design

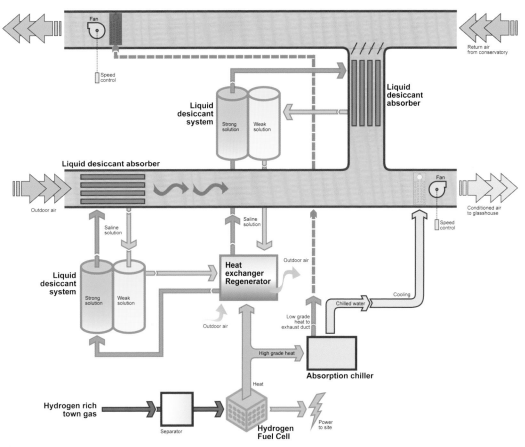

The result is drier air (reduced from 90% to 30% RH) and a 'weak' or dilute solution that is pumped to a series of 'regenerator' units located beneath the Silver Supertree cluster adjacent to the lake. These remove the moisture from the solution by treating it with waste heat supplied from the energy centre, and return it to the strong desiccant tank where it can be re-used for further dehumidification. The exhaust air from the regenerators is discharged through the Supertrees within the Silver cluster back to the atmosphere. A great benefit of this process is that it is possible to effectively store "potential" energy in the form of liquid desiccant to help balance supply and demand and the weak and strong desiccant can be moved through the process at a rate to suit the available supply of thermal energy for regeneration.

A key early ambition was to somehow use the solar energy entering the domes as a part of the 'virtuous' energy cycle. The displacement conditioning arrangement causes the air at the top of the biomes to be significantly warmer than the design temperature at low level, particularly in periods of high solar gain. Air is extracted from the top of the Flower Dome and is returned through an underground tunnel to the adjacent Silver Supertree cluster where it becomes the supply air for the desiccant regenerator equipment. The temperature and dryness of this extracted air increases the efficiency of the system and effectively means that there is an indirect solar energy component to the regeneration process.

opposite The desiccant dehumidification units in the Flower Dome reduce the relative humidity of the incoming air from 90% to 30% in normal operation

above Heat exchangers in the liquid desiccant plant room beneath the Lake cluster. The waste heat from the biomass cycle is used to drive off the moisture extracted from the outdoor air

ENERGY GENERATION & THE ENERGY CENTRE

ENERGY GENERATION & THE ENERGY CENTRE

The high-temperature hot water downstream of the turbine is used to drive absorption chillers which generate chilled water for the dome cooling systems and the desiccant regenerator units.

above Eco-wise model of the biomass boiler plant

In the early stages of the project, the intention was to generate the heat to regenerate the desiccant using solar thermal panels integrated into the Supertrees. This would have been in addition to the heat in the recycled air from the top of the biomes. As the work progressed on the concept design in 2007, research with the Client identified a much more significant waste stream that could possibly meet the energy requirements of the project. NParks are responsible for carefully maintaining the trees that line the streets of Singapore; there are reported to be more than three million of them and each is pruned every 2-3 years, yielding a significant daily quantity of hardwood waste.

The design thus developed around the use of a large biomass boiler (7.2MW) to utilise this waste wood stream to raise superheated, high-pressure steam. This waste wood is chipped and mixed with packing case waste from the nearby freight terminal but is otherwise unprocessed; it is delivered to site by a number of trucks each night and held in a large biomass store with a 'walking floor' that feeds the wood waste into the boiler feed hopper. The steam from the boiler feeds a steam turbine which generates 1 MW of electrical energy which in turn is fed into the site power network. The high-temperature hot water downstream

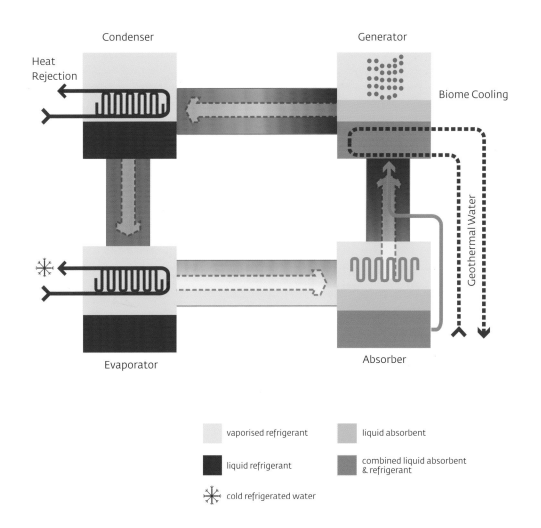

vaporised refrigerant

liquid refrigerant

cold refrigerated water

liquid absorbent

combined liquid absorbent & refrigerant

above An absorption chiller allows waste heat to be used to generate cooling

above Watercooled electric chillers in the energy centre

left The fuel at the heart of the energy cycle - chipped horticultural waste in the biomass store. Up to 15 truck loads a day are needed to drive the energy generation, cooling and desiccant cycles

The Marina Bay South ecosystem

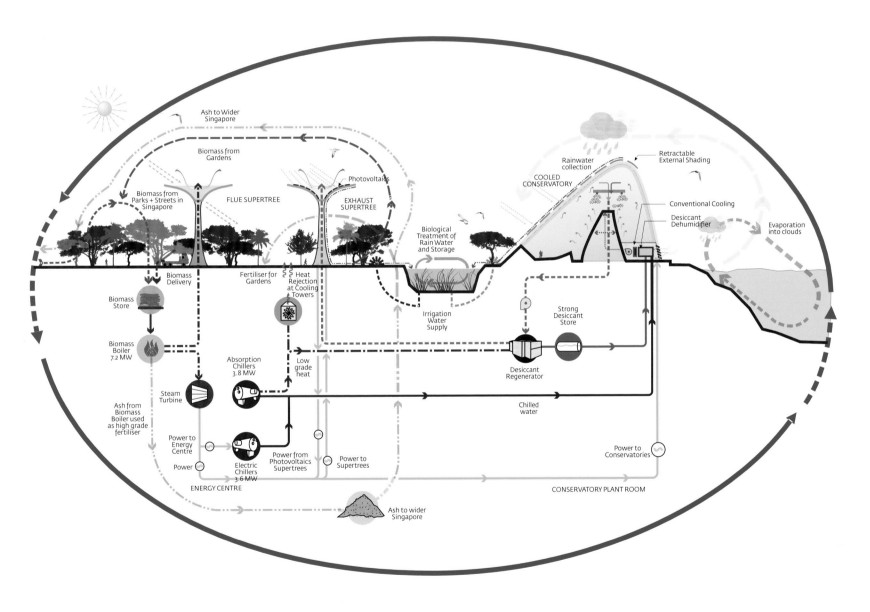

Ash to Wider Singapore

Biomass from Gardens

Biomass from Parks + Streets in Singapore

FLUE SUPERTREE

Photovoltaics

EXHAUST SUPERTREE

Rainwater collection

Retractable External Shading

COOLED CONSERVATORY

Conventional Cooling

Desiccant Dehumidifier

Evaporation into clouds

Biomass Delivery

Fertiliser for Gardens

Heat Rejection at Cooling Towers

Biological Treatment of Rain Water and Storage

Biomass Store

Biomass Boiler 7.2 MW

Absorption Chillers 3.8 MW

Low grade heat

Irrigation Water Supply

Strong Desiccant Store

Steam Turbine

Desiccant Regenerator

Ash from Biomass Boiler used as high grade fertiliser

Power to Energy Centre

Power

Electric Chillers 3.6 MW

Power from Photovoltaics Supertrees

Power to Supertrees

Chilled water

Power to Conservatories

ENERGY CENTRE

CONSERVATORY PLANT ROOM

Ash to wider Singapore

The horticultural waste from the tree pruning was being landfilled before this arrangement was established and so the process effectively turns a waste stream into an active energy supply that displaces the carbon emissions from utility energy.

of the turbine is used to drive absorption chillers, which generate chilled water for the dome cooling systems and the desiccant regenerator units.

The biomass boiler and steam turbine do not modulate easily and the desiccant regeneration load fluctuates with time, so a balancing heat dump was required to stabilise the system. The absorption chillers perform this function while providing useful cooling energy output. The electrical power from the turbine is used to power conventional centrifugal chillers which meet the additional cooling requirements of the biomes at peak periods. At other times, the electrical energy is used to power fans and pumps and any remainder is fed into the site-wide power grid.

The dehumidification load is dependent upon the external conditions and varies throughout the day. The large pipes between the desiccant regenerators and dehumidifiers provide storage of the strong desiccant solution and act as a buffer in addition to a $40m^3$ storage vessel. The desiccant stores energy in the form of latent heat, the strong solution effectively stores about ten times as much energy as an equivalent volume of chilled water. This storage allows for internal load buffering to the system.

The horticultural waste from the tree pruning was being landfilled before this arrangement was established and so the process effectively turns a waste stream into an active energy supply that displaces the carbon emissions from utility energy.

The biomass boiler and turbine system was procured on a 'Design, Build & Operate' basis and the operator selected by NParks, Eco-Wise, completed the installation in late 2011.

above Circulating pumps and motor control panels in the energy centre

right The automatic stokers feeding biomass fuel into the boiler furnace

Ecowise estimate that daily usage at full capacity requires 1,250 cubic metres or 14-16 large transport containers to meet demand. These are delivered each night to the energy centre.

Surplus heat from the CHP and absorption chiller system is rejected from cooling towers located on the upper level of the energy centre. These are the only components of the technical plant that are visible from overlooking buildings and the Supertrees, but even these have been carefully landscaped.

The chilled water circuits that feed the biomes are supplied from the energy centre via the main service tunnel. The temperature at which the water is supplied is varied to suit the external conditions and the required internal conditions. The chilled water temperature is reduced at night during the 'ignition' period for the plants but is elevated during the day to supply the air handling units that supply the displacement systems and floor cooling. Because the desiccants are used to dry the air there is no need for the very cold chilled water during the day time operation that would normally be required for dehumidification in a cooling and reheating process, resulting in significant carbon and energy savings.

The biomass boilers produce two ash streams as a by-product. The first is a fine ash that is high in nitrates and other fertiliser compounds. This ash, once mixed with organic plant waste matter from the gardens, creates a high-quality fertilizer. The second stream of ash contains heavier density particles and is taken off-site to be mixed into concrete or aggregates for the construction industry.

left Cable trays and piping line the walls of the main service tunnel between the energy centre and the domes

opposite In the service tunnel looking back towards the energy centre. The primary pipework and cabling distribution routes are located to the side of the roadway

Gardens By The Bay Biomes
Annual Carbon Evaluation

Annual Carbon Consumption or Offset
[kg CO_2/Year]

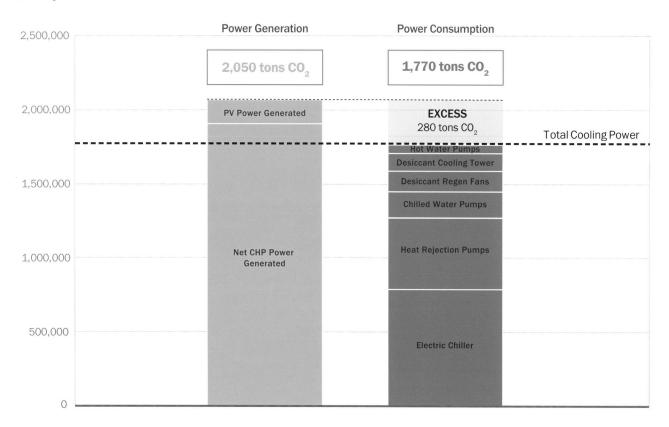

This graph is a comparison of the carbon emissions from the cooling systems for conditioning the biomes with the displaced carbon from on-site renewable energy generation. It indicates that the cooling systems for the biome complex are 'carbon positive' in operation

above On the lower-level of the Flower Dome, in the background the supply air registers on the back wall of the dome, in the foreground a typical environmental measuring station with temperature, humidity and light level sensing

Sensing equipment and controls

Every zone of the biome includes a significant amount of environmental sensing and telemetry including temperature, humidity, radiant temperature and light level sensors to control all aspects of the thermal, radiant and visual environment. The sensors feed information back to control rooms within each biome and to the central control room in the energy centre.

Within these command and control rooms a fully automated Building Management System (BMS) controls all the equipment to monitor conditions and manage equipment. The shading system includes a self-learning algorithm to ensure the system responds to 'real world experiences' of conditions. The combined effort of the biomass CHP and PV systems is to make the provision of cooling to the exhibition spaces within the biomes effectively carbon neutral.

SUPERTREES

DESIGNING WITH NATURE & TECHNOLOGY

SUPERTREES
DESIGNING WITH NATURE & TECHNOLOGY

above The main Supertree cluster in the Lion Grove. The 50m tree in the centre of the cluster houses a fully functional bar on two levels. We like to think of it as the "200 Club" bar. The aerial walkway is accessed from halfway up this Supertree

opposite The three supertrees in the Entry Plaza with the Cloud Forest in the background. The Supertree on the left contains the flue from the biomass boiler

At the heart of the gardens are the Supertrees. These huge structures are a fusion of design, nature and technology. Andrew Grant describes them as "evoking science-fiction and yet tangible and real; enormous and expressive in scale, form and colour". They are a landscape counterpoint to the conservatories and the main cluster holds the centre of the garden, while two smaller clusters frame the main entrance and the lake edge to the south-east. Each of the clusters also performs a distinct environmental function and the Supertrees provide an armature for ducts, flues, shafts and pipes to help remove all evidence of engineering services from the skyline.

The iconic Supertrees are concrete and steel structures formed with a hollow concrete core surrounded by a diaphanous steel cladding which holds the colourful and extensive vertical planting. Seven of the Supertrees contain photovoltaic solar panels on top of the sloped head element. Although the optimal angle for solar collectors in Singapore is effectively horizontal, the head of the tree is constructed to include a slight fall to allow for a degree of self-cleaning by rainfall.

The Supertree cluster closest to the main entrance, the Gold Cluster, is also close to the energy centre. Within the Gold Cluster, one of the 37m Supertrees conceals the main chimney from the boilers. The chimney is required to discharge at a high level to ensure that none of the products of combustion are visible at plaza level and that the flue gases are dispersed well above the occupied piazza. An extensive flue gas scrubbing system in the boiler house of the energy centre uses multiple processes including an electrostatic precipitator to ensure that atmospheric emissions are invisible, harmless and non-toxic. The installation of the carbon steel flue into the Supertree was a significant construction operation as it was installed as a single element, craned into position inside the already erected concrete core of the Supertree in a very delicate operation with little tolerance.

The Silver Cluster of Supertrees at the Dragonfly lake edge, closest to the Marina Bay Sands Hotel, contains the discharges from the regeneration unit of the liquid desiccant dehumidificatic system. Hot air from the top of the Flower Dome is routed throug a duct to a plant room at the base of the trees, where it is drawn through desiccant regeneration units. These units heat the air further using waste heat from the biomass boiler and effectively remove the moisture that has been captured from the incoming air as part of the dehumidification process (in a process similar to boiling the moisture out of the salt solution). The hot moist air th generated is ducted up the centre of the Supertrees to discharge t_ the atmosphere at over 30 metres above the ground.

The largest of the Supertrees towers 50 metres above the Supertree Grove in the centre of the garden and contains a two-storey bar and public viewing gallery. This large Supertree is extensively serviced for public occupation and contains a double helix staircase wrapped around the central core, ingeniously providing two means of escape.

An important function of any tree or vertical element in a tropical garden is the provision of shade and the Supertrees were also designed with a view to providing extensive areas of shade to the publicly accessed facilities in the Supertree Grove.

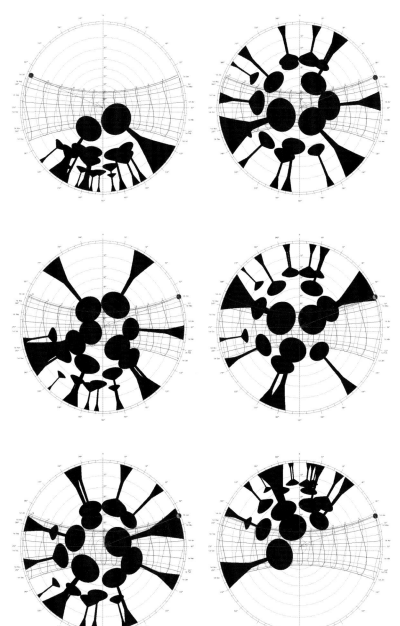

right The diagram shows an early study that looked at the sunpaths and mapped the areas of light and shade from the Supertrees in the Lion Grove Plaza

opposite Photosynthetically active radiation, PAR study showing varying levels of direct sunlight falling on the differing surfaces of the Supertrees and surrounding landscape

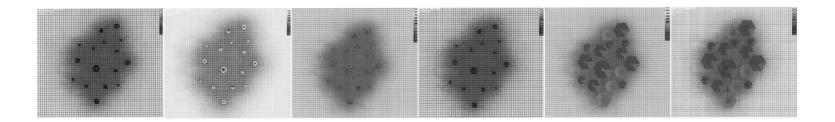

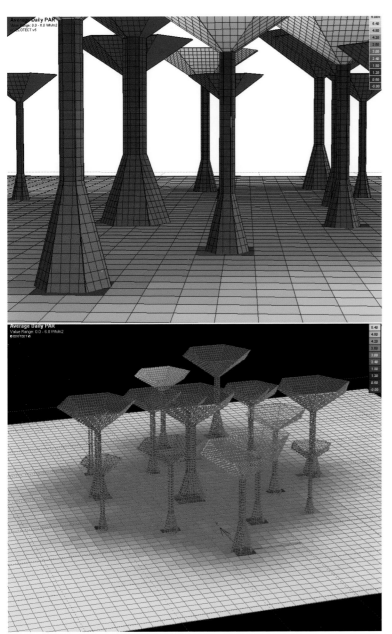

Finally, the Supertrees contain an extensive array of lighting equipment which transform the gardens at night into a magical destination for the public and increase the visibility and sense of wonder when this extraordinary garden is viewed from near and far.

To quote Andrew Grant once again "in time, the true rainforest trees planted in the gardens will reach the heights of these structures and become equal wonders of the project. Until then, the Supertrees provide a unique skyline to the site and to the changing city context of Singapore".

The extraordinary engineering feat that is represented by the Supertrees is the work of our brilliant colleagues at Atelier One. Neil Thomas describes them as "beautiful symbols for the gardens, otherworldly. The structures are doubly curved anticlastic surfaces using form to create stiffness. The work to get them approved, or even understood, was challenging, yet somehow they look effortless".

AFTERWORD

A question that we are sometimes asked is whether constructing such significant gardens, public realm and buildings to create artificial environments in the climate of Singapore can ever be described as a 'sustainable' proposition? While this question could be asked of any project that involves the development of something new, the nature of the Gardens by the Bay scheme meant that this question was at the forefront of our collective minds throughout the process and we continually sought to find ways to reduce the environmental impact of the project.

As environmental designers we are frequently faced with a brief that seeks sustainable outcomes from the delivery of the building or buildings for a predetermined purpose that we cannot control. In these situations, we believe that it falls to us to make the most of the resources at our disposal both from the local climate and environment. In addition, we must endeavour to not just "do more with less" as Buckminster Fuller would have said but to seek out and initiate virtuous cycles where the development of the project can be beneficial to the local environment and not just less bad.

Within the integrated and highly complex processes and systems that have been instigated for the Gardens by the Bay there is a level of rigour to the sustainable thinking that sets it apart as an exemplar for buildings in the region and around the world. It will be seen by tens of millions of people and will become a beacon for applied sustainable design in the region. No doubt many of the technologies that have been described in the foregoing chapters have been individually applied to buildings in Asia. However, it was the recognition by everybody involved in the project that integrated design, which requires considerable ingenuity and the painstaking application of multiple incremental design solutions, is what makes this project truly exceptional in both aspiration and realisation.

A project like Gardens by the Bay comes along perhaps once-in-a-lifetime if you're very lucky. We consider ourselves to have been blessed to have had the opportunity to work on something so spectacular and ultimately so wonderful.

Atelier Ten
London
August 2012

opposite The gardens from the Barrage with the Marina Bay Sands complex in the background

CONTRIBUTORS

CONTRIBUTORS

Patrick Bellew RDI
Founding Director, Atelier Ten
BSc (Hons) FREng HonFRIBA CEng FCIBSE
FEI FRSA MASHRAE

Founding director of Atelier Ten (1991), Patrick is one of the UK's Royal Designers and is a Chartered Building Services Engineer with more than thirty years' experience in the design of high-performance buildings and systems. With extensive experience in the integration of environmental and building systems with architecture, Patrick has particular expertise in thermal-mass energy storage technologies and high-efficiency building conditioning systems. Patrick's success in integrating innovative technologies with noteworthy architecture has been acknowledged by the Royal Institute of British Architects, who made him an Honorary Fellow in 2001. Patrick was elected a Fellow of the Royal Academy of Engineering in 2004. He has taught at Yale University School of Architecture since 2000 and has twice been the Eero Saarinen Visiting Professor.

Patrick was one of the original group who founded the UK-Green Building Council in 2006 and was a member of the Executive Board from 2006 - 2010 when the organisation became a registered charity. He now serves on the Trustee Board. In 2008 Patrick delivered the 6th Happold Medal Lecture and received the Happold Medal from the Construction Industry Council and the Happold Foundation.

He is on the Awards panel for the 2012 - 2015 RIBA Awards and is on the Judging panel for the World Architecture Awards 2012.

Meredith Davey
Senior Associate Director, Atelier Ten
BSc (Hons), Graduate Certificate, CEnv,
CEng, MEI, LEED APTM, bd+ctm

Meredith Davey joined Atelier Ten in 2005 and has worked on a series of international projects with an emphasis on high-performance design, energy efficiency and sustainability. As a Senior Associate Director, Meredith leads the UK Environmental Design Practice. Alongside delivering building design, Meredith delivers bespoke services that include advanced computational analysis covering daylighting, thermal and energy & carbon modelling and financial modelling including payback analysis & net present value analysis. Within this role he has also developed R&D studies including analysis of differing building typologies to assess their environmental impact. An example would include working with a large European Insurer to develop analytical and cost models for low-carbon renovation and retrofit across their European Property portfolio.

Meredith regularly gives public and educational talks throughout the world and has contributed to numerous publications. He has been a Visiting Lecturer in the MSc in Intelligent Buildings program at Reading University since 2009. Meredith is a member of the Energy Institute and is also a Chartered Engineer and a Chartered Environmentalist. Meredith was appointed a Design Council/ CABE Built Environment Expert in 2012.

Andrew Grant
Founding Director, Grant Associates
BA (Hons), CMLI, Hon FRIBA

Paul Baker
Director, Wilkinson Eyre Architects
BA (Hons) DipArch ARB RIBA

Neil Thomas
Founding Director, Atelier One

Andrew formed Grant Associates in 1997 to explore the emerging frontiers of landscape architecture within sustainable development. His approach is driven by a fascination with creative ecology and the promotion of quality and innovation in project work. He has built up experience in all scales and types of projects from sub-regional planning to the detailing of the smallest piece of new landscapes.

He is a member of CABE Space and the South West Regional Design Panel.

Paul Baker joined Wilkinson Eyre Architects in 1990 and has been a Director since 1999. He has a particular interest in holistic design, and specifically how architecture can be integrated into its context across the disciplines of urban design, landscape architecture, planning and environment. He has an enthusiasm for designing buildings which contribute to long-term sustainability and regeneration, and which reinforce an experiential narrative for users. This approach made leadership of the Singapore Gardens by the Bay project particularly fitting to his expertise, which also includes cultural and commercial buildings for clients such as The Science Museum in London and the Royal Botanic Gardens at Kew. Paul believes that the best architecture is a result of inventiveness and creativity but also tenacity. For him, the final built project should retain the vitality and excitement of the initial concept sketch.

Paul was a CABE (Commission for Architecture and the Built Environment) Enabler from 2001 to 2007 and within the Practice he leads design review and heads the Sustainability Unit, which he established in 2004.

Neil Thomas is the Director of Atelier One, which has been described as 'the most innovative engineering practice in the UK'.

Atelier One has gained an international reputation as a Structural Engineering Practice specialising in challenging projects. Collaborations with Architects, Artists and Designers have resulted in many interesting built projects such as Federation Square, Melbourne with LAB + Bates Smart, Cloud Gate with Anish Kapoor, Stages for U2's 360 Degree World Tour & The Queen's Diamond Jubilee with Mark Fisher and the Opening Ceremony for the London 2012 Olympics.

Neil holds a number of high-profile posts in the UK & US educational service, most recently being a Visiting Professor to Yale, and has recently co-written a book titled 'Liquid Threshold' which gives insight to the complex challenges of a number of extraordinary projects.

GREEN:HOUSE GREEN:ENGINEERING

ACKNOWLEDGEMENTS

The many people to be thanked include the following key members of the Atelier Ten team who were instrumental in the delivery of the project:

Ajay Shah
Chris Edwards
Chris Grubb
Corinna Gage
Des Kenny
Elaine Mitchell
Emma Marchant
Greg Thomas
Guy Clay
Kerri Marshall
Leanne Renn
Ludwig Abache
Mark Smith
Michela Mangiarotti
Mike Hammock
Nerissa Mauricio
Nigel Horan
Pamela Lewis
Paul Christou
Piers Watts-Jones
Preena Patel
Rudolph Duncan-Bosu
Seohaa Lucas-Choi
Uma Sardana

CONSULTANTS AND MAIN CONTRACTORS OF THE GARDENS BY THE BAY PROJECT

Project Management
PM Link Pte Ltd

Consultants
Atelier One Structural Engineers
Atelier Ten Building Services Engineers
CPG Consultants Pte Ltd Executive Architectural, Executive Mechanical & Electrical Engineers, Executive Civil & Structural Engineers, and Quantity Surveyors
Davis Langdon & Seah Quantity Surveyor (Singapore Office)
Grant Associates Masterplanner and Landscape Architect
Land Design Studio Interpretative Consultants
Lighting Planners Associates Inc Lighting Design Consultants
Meinhardt Infrastructure Pte Ltd Civil & Structural Engineers
Speirs & Major Lighting Design Consultants
Thomas.Matthews Graphic Design and Identity
Wilkinson Eyre Architects Architect

Contractors
Ecowise Holdings Ltd
Expand Construction Pte Ltd
Koon Construction & Transport Co Pte Ltd
Planar One & Associates Pte Ltd
Precise Development Pte Ltd
Swee Hong Engineering Construction Pte Ltd
Taiki-Sha Ltd
Who Hup Pte Ltd

GLOSSARY OF TERMS

Desiccant

A substance that has a high affinity for water and is used as a drying agent. In solid form, the material is usually calcium oxide or silica gel: in liquid form (as at Gardens by the Bay) lithium chloride is used.

Sensible heat (Q)

Heat exchanged in a thermodynamic system that has the sole effect of a change in temperature. It is calculated by the product of the bodies mass (M) with its specific heat capacity (Cp) and the temperature change (ΔT).

$Q = M.Cp.\Delta T$

Latent Heat

The heat exchanged in a thermodynamic system during a process that occurs without a change of temperature. A good example would be the changes in energy that occur at a change in state such as ice forming or melting or the boiling of water. Latent heat transfer also occurs at a change in moisture content in a system.

Enthalpy

The total heat content of a substance (in this case normally air) per unit mass. Enthalpy in air-conditioning applications is made up of Sensible (dry) and Latent (moisture) heat energy.

Technically $H = U + PV$

where H = enthalpy (kg/kg)

U = Internal Energy

P = Pressure

V = Volume

Lux

The SI unit of illuminance, this is a measure of luminous flux per unit area (lumens/m$_2$) or the measure of visible light intensity on a surface. The unit is weighted to human perception by weighting each wavelength according to the luminosity function (a standardised modal of human visual brightness perception).

Lux-hours

The measure of luminous exposure over time on a surface. At Gardens by the Bay the design work included calculation of the annual luminous exposure of all parts of the glasshouses. The units used are Mlux hours or '000,000's of lux hours per year. (This measure is frequently used by Museum curators to control the exposure of artefacts to natural light.)

Dehumidification

The process of removing moisture from the air before it is distributed into a building or space. Typically this is achieved by passing moist air over a cold surface such as a cooling coil. This causes dehumidification through condensation. At Gardens by the Bay most of the dehumidification is achieved using liquid desiccants which is more efficient where there is a renewable or waste heat source.

Absorption Refrigeration

A process that uses a heat source (e.g. solar or waste heat from combined heat and power plants) to provide the energy to drive a cooling system. Invented by French scientist Ferdinand Carré in 1858, absorption refrigerators use a refrigerant such as lithium bromide or ammonia with a very low boiling point (<-18°C) and pass it through a three phase cycle of evaporation, absorption and regeneration to deliver cooling from heat.

At Gardens by the Bay, the absorption chillers in the main energy centre use waste heat from the turbine to generate chilled water. Surplus heat is rejected at the Cooling Towers.

Cooling Towers

Heat removal devices used to transfer waste heat from a process to the atmosphere. Usually located at roof level, these machines reject unwanted heat through a process of evaporation to cool the working fluid.

Turbine

A turbine generates circular motion when a fluid is passed over it. At Gardens by the Bay, the fluid used is superheated high-pressure steam, with the energy from the pressure of the steam used to generate motion. This mechanical action is turned into electrical power through an alternator (effectively a motor working in reverse) and in Gardens by the Bay this generates 1,000kW (or 1MW) of electrical power.

Photovoltaic Cell

A photovoltaic cell generates electricity by converting sunlight into power. The Photovoltaic effect was first observed in 1839 Alexandre-Edmond Becquerel. In Gardens by the Bay, the photovoltaics are formed from mono-crystalline silicon cells, which are doped semi-conductor grade silicon. When a particle of light, a photon, hits the silicon it causes an electron to become excited and thereby generates an electrical flow.

Stratification

Stratification is where hot air rises within a volume forming a number of layers of constant temperatures. These stratified layers increase in temperature with height as warmer air is less dense and therefore has relative buoyancy compared to colder air in the same space. The density of air is governed by the following equation:

$P = P \div (R . T)$, where
P is density
p is absolute pressure
R is the specific gas constant
T is absolute temperature

Displacement Ventilation

Displacement ventilation systems introduce cooled air to a space at low level and at low velocity, as opposed to conventional air conditioning systems, which rely on injecting air at high-level and high-speed. Displacement ventilation removes heat and contaminants by displacing them as the air warms and rises, and thus allows tall spaces to be cooled only at the bottom.

Spectrally Selective Glazing and Selectivity

Spectrally selective glazing allows solar radiation of only certain wavelengths through it by the application of a low-e tin oxide coating. The selectivity ratio is the ratio between how much of the suns original visual light is transmitted compared to how much of the suns original solar energy (or heat) is transmitted. The glass used in the conservatoires for Gardens by the Bay allows 64% of the light through, while only allowing 38% of the solar energy though, resulting in a selectivity ratio of 1.7, which is close to the theoretical maximum.

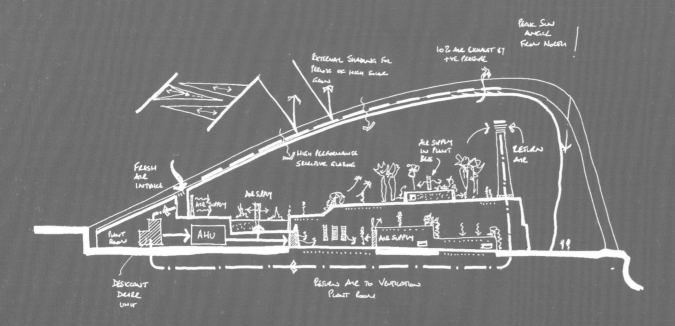